CULTURE SHOCK!

Burma

Saw Myat Yin

Compliments
of
Family Liaison

Graphic Arts Center Publishing Company
Portland, Oregon

In the same series

Australia	Indonesia	Philippines	
Borneo	Israel	Singapore	
Britain	Japan	South Africa	
Canada	Korea	Spain	
China	Malaysia	Sri Lanka	
France	Nepal	Thailand	
India	Pakistan	USA	

Forthcoming

Hong Kong
Italy
Norway
Taiwan

Illustrations by TRIGG
Cover photographs from APA
Photographs from Image Bank and Ellis Klarenbeek

© 1994 Times Editions Pte Ltd

This book is published by special
arrangement with Times Editions Pte Ltd
International Standard Book Number 1-55868-148-5
Graphic Arts Center Publishing Company
P.O. Box 10306 • Portland, Oregon 97210 • (503) 226-2402

Printed in Singapore

To my parents and teachers
with gratitude,
and to my family
with love.

CONTENTS

Introduction *6*
Acknowledgements *8*

1 Burma Profile *9*
2 A Lifetime of Ceremony *31*
3 Burmese Perceptions *54*
4 Getting To Know The Burmese *69*
5 Visiting and Entertaining *111*
6 Travelling Inside Burma *145*
7 Settling In *157*
8 Doing Business in Burma *179*

Cultural Quiz *194*
Glossary *200*
Further Reading *202*
The Author *204*
Index *205*

INTRODUCTION

Unlike most of the other books in the *Culture Shock* series, *Culture Shock Burma* is not written by an expatriate who has lived in the country described but by a native of that place. What is presented is a description of certain points of sensitivity for the foreigner, but from an insider's perspective. Consequently, it was with some trepidation that I undertook the task of writing this book for fear of a native familiarity causing me to miss the wood for the trees (or vice versa).

To balance the description as far as possible, questionnaires were sent out to a sample of people who had lived in or, more commonly, had visited Burma. Foreigners who have lived in Burma for longer periods are mainly diplomatic corps personnel and United Nations staff, many of whom were not readily accessible. Thus, anecdotal evidence is supplied where questionnaires could not be used. Such examples help to describe possible difficulties, situations and things to look out for.

A large number of expatriate Burmese now live abroad in places like Australia, the USA, the UK and Canada. Those of Burmese background, rather than of Chinese or Indian descent, are likely to cling to Burmese values and lifestyles where possible, at least among the older generation. Complaints of children being rude to elders and wanting to have their own way are frequent, as is the common lament over children being unable to speak or read Burmese. Therefore, this book may serve to guide not only those who are intending to visit and live in Burma, but also those who are in contact with expatriate Burmese all over the world.

For those who have visited, Burma often holds a mystique and intangible beauty. In an age when the rest of the world is full of machines, industries and manufactured consumer products, Burma's lack of economic development is responsible for much of the beautiful unspoiled landscape and the feeling of timelessness the land evokes. It is partly because of this that I have chosen to use the name Burma in this book, although the country has been called Myanmar since 1989. Most people are familiar with the old name, while Myanmar is relatively new and does not yet hold the same romantic, golden and timeless images that the name Burma does. Moreover, much of the available literature on Burma is from a time past (namely the 1950s and 1960s) and refers to the old names of towns and cities. By comparison, that of recent years has concentrated specifically on the country's political situation which has received world-wide attention.

Because of the latter, there may be some reason to doubt the need for a book of the present nature, since Burma still remains somewhat closed to foreigners. At best it is only marginally accessible compared to the period before the *coup d'etat* of 1988. Nevertheless, it seems that no country can remain completely closed as the world gets smaller due to more efficient communication and transport systems. Besides, Burma's beauty and relatively forgotten nature can only increase future interest, whether this interest stems from business motivations or otherwise .

Culture Shock Burma may be before its time but it is hoped that such a time will not be too far in the future as to make this book meaningless.

ACKNOWLEDGEMENTS

My sincere thanks to Ms Shirley Hew for making this book possible through her friendship and large doses of encouragement. My thanks and appreciation to Ms Patricia Herbert for helping me with the questionnaires, and to all the respondents who shared their experiences and gave me much useful information. To Joanne Riccioni, my editor, thank you for your great patience in working on the manuscript and putting it all together.

All errors and omissions in subject matter are my own. Any additional information or corrections are welcome through the publishers.

— Chapter One —

BURMA PROFILE

"It is only with time, with the growth of sympathy, that the charm and beauty of the palace steal on one."

—V.C. Scott Q'Connor,
Mandalay and Other Cities of the Past in Burma.

The above quotation refers to Mandalay Palace but the same sentiment seems to apply to Burma itself. Many visitors have said that the charm of Burma steals on one, although it may not be on the first visit.

Visiting Burma for the first time or staying there for longer periods can present something of a shock. One Burma-watcher was said to have exclaimed, "Burma seems to have been set in aspic, it is so unchanging!" In other words, things were almost exactly the same as when he last saw the country more than 40 years ago. Others have described it as a journey back through a time tunnel or a time warp as time in Burma seems to have stopped somewhere in the early 1900s. Visitors from places like Singapore and Malaysia often see in present-day Burma the look and lifestyle their own countries had at the turn of the century.

Burma usually evokes "golden memories" for those who lived there prior to the 1950s. This description may have literally been inspired by the golden-spired pagodas that dot the whole country, or by the fact that the Burmese refer to their country as *Shway Pyi Daw* (The Golden Land), "golden" being an honorific for a beloved object. In reality, such golden memories refer to a time of comparative prosperity when money had value and many goods and services were available locally.

Lately a number of books have referred to the country as "The Forgotten Land", which Burma has indeed become because of its isolation and closed nature. Many people (even Asians) have only a vague idea of where Burma is located, despite the fact that the country occupies a very large area of land between two of the world's most heavily populated countries - India and China.

Later visitors and those staying longer either love or hate life in Burma. The lack of basic amenities, such as regular water and electricity; the lack of consumer goods found in more developed countries; and the complete absence of nightlife, even in the capital city, are cause enough for foreign residents to find living in Burma a great inconvenience.

Yet those who do love it will praise the fresh air, the fresh vegetables and fruit, and the green trees, although it is true that the latter are nowadays diminishing in number. The secret is that these residents have learnt to get the best of both worlds by enjoying the advantages of underdevelopment, while taking frequent shopping trips to cities in neighbouring countries to get what they need in terms of consumer goods.

There is no doubt that some Burmese are also able to enjoy a lifestyle that would be the envy of people in developed countries. When earnings can be obtained in foreign exchange many Burmese are able to buy consumer goods on the black market, hire servants and own several cars and houses. Of course, such people form a minority group and most Burmese struggle to maintain a normal existence amidst economic instability.

Because Burma is a little-known country, we shall start off with a brief survey, touching on its people, geography, history and economy.

PEOPLE

Burma has been described as an anthropologist's dream by some writers as it possesses such a great a diversity of ethnic groups with distinct dress, customs and traditions. According to the 1983 Census, the distribution of these groups was as follows:

Burmese	69%
Shan	8.5%
Karen	6.2%
Arakanese	4.5%
Other indigenous races	6.5%
Mixed Burmese and foreign races	1.3%
Chinese	0.7%
Indians and Pakistanis	1.4%
Foreigners	1.9%

While the largest groups of Burmese live mainly in the river valleys and plains, many of the smaller ethnic minorities live in the mountains and hills, seldom venturing into the urban areas because of the poor communications infrastructure. In fact, many highland people have never visited the lowlands and vice versa.

Consequently, products and materials from one region do not reach other parts of the country, so are little-known and not part of the normal consumption patterns there. This lack of communication serves to enhance the diversity of lifestyles, customs and habits amongst the people of Burma. For instance grapefruit juice, which is made in the Kachin state and is available in the capital, Rangoon (now Yangon), might not be consumed in the far south of Burma as it cannot be transported that far. To take advantage of the greatest variety of consumer goods, those who can go to Rangoon periodically for a shopping spree.

Ethnic Groups

The peoples who settled in what is now known as Burma came in three waves of migration. The first migration brought the Mon and the Khmer, the second group were Tibeto-Burman and the third consisted of the Tai-Chinese people who settled in the area in the 13th and 14th centuries.

The ethnic Burmese who form the majority of the population are the descendants of the Burmans, Mon and the Tai-Chinese. They are predominantly Buddhist. However the great diversity of ethnic peoples who make up the rest of the population may be divided into eight main groups. These are the Kachin, Karen (or Kayin), Kayah (or Red Karen), Shan (or Tai), Chin, Myanmar, Mon and Arakanese (or Rakhine). There are, moreover, many sub-groups within these main groups. Generally, the first five races are distinct in dress, traditions and culture, while the last three are more or less homogenous in appearance and dress, but have their own languages. Most of the ethnic races are named after the areas in which they live, often the mountain and hill regions towards the borders of the country.

The Mon and the Arakanese are closely related to the Burmese, being tall and dark in appearance, practising Buddhism and living mainly as farmers. On the other hand, the Karen, who form two groups called the Sgaw and Pwo Karen, are often Christian and tend to have a fairer colouring and more stocky build. The Shan are related to the people of Thailand, Laos, Cambodia and Vietnam. They are usually tall and fair. Mainly farmers, they live in the river valleys and lowland pockets of the Shan plateau.

The Chin people live in the Chin states and are dark in complexion, while the Kachin live in the Kachin state in the northernmost part of Burma and tend to have a fair colouring but broad features. What links these groups is that both still practice animism, although some have been converted to Christianity by missionaries in their areas. These two tribes are also famed for their fierce fighting spirit.

As well as these ethnic races, you may also come across many Sino-Burmese or Indo-Burmese, the result of intermarriage between Burmese and the large numbers of migrants from neighbouring India and China.

While I have outlined some of the more common characteristics and features of the main ethnic minorities in Burma, one should, however, be wary of jumping to conclusions based on these. There are many other smaller ethnic groups, many of which have their own distinctive features, customs and dress. Some of these smaller ethnic races are the Palaung, Padaung, Lisu, Wa, Danu, Lahu, Lashi and Yaw.

The most famous of these is perhaps the Padaung who live in the Kayah state. While this community form only a tiny proportion of the population, they have become well-known because of tourism posters which show their women wearing heavy brass neck rings, perhaps fuelling the misconception that the practice is common amongst Burmese women. Actually, this tribal custom is said to be a deliberate deformation of the womenfolk so that they will not be taken by other tribes.

Ethnic War

Sadly, ethnic wars amongst the people of Burma have gone on from the time that independence was gained and there are no signs of the bitterness diminishing. Initially, these wars were instigated by the breaching of the Panglong Agreement of 1947, which stated that the main ethnic groups had a right to secede if they wished to after independence was gained. Now, over forty years later, various ethnic races continue to fight over their right to autonomy, but also add discrimination, economic underdevelopment and even revenue distribution to their list of grievances. Large numbers of losses on all sides seem to have had little effect as a deterrent and over the years Burma has suffered from all the destruction and instability that warfare brings.

Peace would have brought much greater prosperity to the people much sooner but goals have been focused on political union rather than on economic development. Nevertheless, a recent cease-fire between the Kachin, Wa, Shan and Pao has opened up many areas which, judging from newspaper reports, may be developed for tourism in the future. Such economic development might be a greater incentive for peace.

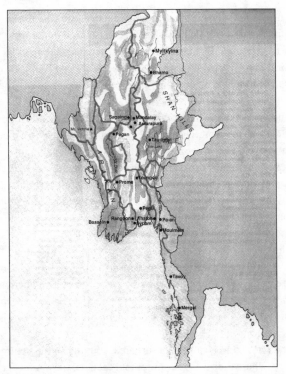

GEOGRAPHY

Burma occupies a large land area of over 676 000 square kilometres. It lies between latitude 10 and 28 degrees north, and longitude 92 and 101 degrees east. Borders are shared with Bangladesh and India in the north-west, China in the north-east, and Laos and Thailand in the south-east. Towards the south and south-west are the Andaman Sea and the Bay of Bengal.

Burma can be divided into distinct zones, namely the northern mountain ranges, the Shan plateau in the east, the central Dry Zone, the river valleys, the Irrawaddy (or Aye yarwaddy) delta and the long Tenasserim (Taninthayi) strip in the south.

The western and northern mountain ranges are very high and form the outer spurs of the Himalayas. There is snow in the most remote parts, though most Burmese have never been to these areas. However, visitors (mainly trekkers from the mountaineering associations) say that the rhododendron and firs found here are a particularly beautiful sight.

The Shan plateau in the east rises about 3000 feet above sea level. The Salween (or Thanlwin) river, which has its source in Tibet, flows down the plateau through very narrow and unnavigable gorges. However, the Irrawaddy is the longest river, beginning in the Himalayas and flowing for some 1300 miles. As well as being a major means of transport, the Irrawaddy's annual flooding during the rainy season makes its rich banks and delta area the most fertile in Burma for paddy farming.

The river valley effectively divides Burma into two areas, the east and west. The eastern area is more densely populated and is connected to the capital and other major towns by road and railway networks. In contrast, the western areas have to be reached by riverboat as there are still no bridges across the river, except for the Ava Bridge near Mandalay.

The Dry Zone is a semi-desert area, roughly in the centre of the country, where thorny trees, shrubs and cacti are the main vegetation. It is in this area that Mandalay and Pagan are located. These two kingdoms of the past are now Burma's most visited cities after the capital.

The Irrawaddy delta is made up of many creeks and streams with banks of alluvial soils suitable for growing rice, the staple of the Burmese diet. Many fish and shrimps are also available in this area and the delta is famous for various types of dried fish, fish and shrimp sauces, and pastes. Here, a typical meal is one of rice, fish paste dip and fresh vegetables (boiled or raw) from the farmer's vegetable patch. Similarly, in the areas where cooking oil is produced, a simple meal would consist of rice mixed with oil and lightly salted.

Fishing on Inle Lake.

The Tenasserim strip that lies towards the south is largely cut off from other parts of the country. In this region there is a long mountain range stretching north to south and a narrow coastal strip. While the land offers tin mines and quarries, the chief economic activity here in recent years has been trade between Thailand, Malaysia and Singapore. However, to reach the most southerly parts, transport has to be by sea or air.

Towns and Cities

There are few large towns in Burma except for the capital and main port, Rangoon. Even this is a quiet and green city with two large lakes and a population density of 1013 people per square mile. After Rangoon, the two main cities are Mandalay and Moulmein (Mawlamyaing). Other towns are relatively small.

Mandalay, the country's main cultural centre, has grown in spite of several fires that razed large parts of the city to the ground. New and finer buildings are currently being built and the talk is that the financial backing behind these ventures comes from a growing class of *nouveau riche* who may possibly be drug-related traders. How true such rumours are is anybody's guess.

Rangoon has also made efforts to spruce up appearances of late. This has included compulsory repainting, walling, fencing and road repairs. Again, many of the community's wealthier members appear to have contributed financially to these projects, which have also included the construction of parks, fountains and small-scale amusement centres.

One should also note that street names in Rangoon are now Burmese rather than English. For example, Windermere Road, a long and winding road named after the English river, is now Thanlwin Road, after the Burmese river. Roads which were spelt according to British phonetics are now spelt the way they would be pronounced in Burmese. For example, Prome Road, one of the longest roads in the city, is now called Pyi Road. After independence, many roads were renamed entirely, so Dalhousie, Fraser and Montgomery Streets became Maha Bandoola, Anawrahta and Bogyoke Aung San Street respectively, after Burma's famous generals. Indeed, you'll probably find an Aung San Street in every Burmese town.

Sadly, many small Burmese towns which were previously quite prosperous by virtue of being located along the railway route, have now sunk into poverty because of the greater use of roads. This has been brought about by the import of large numbers of pick-up trucks which are used for carrying goods and people from one town to another.

Climate

Burma has three seasons: the dry season from March to June; the wet season or monsoon from July to October; and the cool season from November to February.

Climate, of course, varies from region to region due to the country's diverse geography. In the river valleys and delta, including Rangoon, the rainfall is about 254cm (100in) per annum and the average temperature is about 32°C (90°F). The hottest period is in April and May when temperatures can reach about 40°C (104°F), while the coldest is in January when temperatures often fall to 16°C (60°F).

The coastal areas in the west and south have very high rainfall, about 508cm (200in) per annum. In the rainy season this means days and days of continuous rain, unlike Rangoon and the towns south of the dry zone where rain usually alternates with sunny periods. Take note that this continuous rain and the excessive humidity which results tends to cause mildew and fungus on clothes, books and even furniture.

In the Dry Zone temperatures can reach an incredible 46°C (114°F). To cope with such unbearable heat the Burmese have a number of customs and habits. Many will move beds and mattresses outdoors onto pavements, returning to the house in the cool of the early hours; others sleep on mats sprayed with water; while some will bathe in a barrel at regular intervals, or even stay there!

On a visit to Pagan, the author was forced by the stifling heat to join the rest of the town trying to sleep outdoors. Unfortunately, I ended up being awake for most of the night, listening to the conversations of neighbours who had given up on sleep and were spending the night catching up on gossip. This gossip also included reference to a funeral which was being held around the corner, said to be a death caused by bathing at the wrong hour. Because of the high temperatures, the Burmese believe that sickness and even death can be caused by taking baths in the afternoons or after being exposed to the sun.

HISTORICAL MILESTONES

The Burmese are very proud of their history, which dates back to the founding of Pagan (Bagan) in the 9th century A.D. The Burmese Empire was once quite substantial, spreading as far as Assam and Manipur in the west, and as far as Cambodia in the east. The Burmese kings traditionally conceived of themselves and their empire as the centre of the universe and they ruled with absolute power. Later, however, in their dealings with the advancing British, this was to eventually prove their downfall as they did not have enough knowledge or experience of the outside world.

Early History

Early history is shrouded in myth and legend. However, experts believe that the Irrawaddy valley was inhabited 5000 years ago by the Mon who entered from the region now known as Thailand and Cambodia and began to cultivate the land. At roughly the same time, a loosely knit group of tribes known as the Pyu migrated from their Tibetan home and settled in the upper Irrawaddy valley. Excavations show that a great civilization centred around the city of Prome (Pyi). However, the Pyu were defeated by the Mon in the 8th century and the Burmans, who had previously been subject to them, came into prominence.

The First Burmese Empire

The Burmans established their kingdom at Pagan but it was two centuries later, under the rule of King Anawrahta in the 11th century, that the first Burmese Empire was founded. During his reign, the Mon in the south were conquered and most of Burma was united, except for the Shan hills and parts of Arakan and Tenasserim. He also brought the *Tripitaka* to Pagan, thus introducing Buddhism to the Burmans who were previously animists. However, when the kingdom fell to the Mongols in 1287 it disintegrated into small states with the Mon building a new state in Pegu (Bago), the Shan at Ava (Innwa) and the Burmans at Toungoo.

The Second Burmese Empire

The second Burmese Empire was founded by King Bayinnaung between 1551 and 1581. He both regained territories lost by his predecessors and added to them Chiangmai, Ayuthia (now Thailand) and Tenasserim. The capital was moved to Pegu which became an important port for trade with neighbouring countries. Later, in the 17th century, the capital was moved to Ava when the British, Dutch and French trading companies were established in Burma. However, with help from the French, the Mon captured Ava in 1752 and from there tried to control all of the country.

The Third Burmese Empire

It was only after eight years of warfare that the Mon were finally defeated by King Alaungpaya who united the country and formed the third Burmese Empire. His son and successor, Hsinbyushin, successfully invaded neighbouring Siam and destroyed Ayuthia in 1767. It was this conquest which brought the Siamese influence to Burmese arts, dance and music. Hsinbyushin's brother, Bodawpaya, later won Arakan and did much to improve communications, education and the legal system in Burma. The Konbaung Dynasty which this family founded was the last dynasty to rule Burma before the British took it over as a colony.

British Rule

The British annexed Burma in three stages, during the three Anglo-Burmese Wars of 1824, 1852, and 1886. In the first they gained the Arakan and Tenasserim territories; in the second lower Burma was conquered; while the third resulted in the control of Mandalay and upper Burma. The Royal family were then exiled to India.

It was only in the first part of the 20th century that nationalist leaders came into prominence. The most famous was Burma's national hero, Aung San. Starting his political career as a young student at Rangoon University, he developed and led the Thakin Movement, *thakin* (meaning "master") being a term the Burmese had to use when addressing the British. Members of the movement deliberately wore traditional dress, especially jackets made of brown cotton called *pin ni*.

World War Two and Independence

During the Second World War, Aung San formed the Thirty Comrades, a group which resisted British rule and looked to the Japanese for help in training forces to fight them. When the Japanese occupation proved to be cruel and ruthless, the nationalists were forced to move camp and look to the British to help drive them out. The Burma Independence Army finally liberated Burma from the Japanese on 27th March 1945, now known as Armed Forces Day (previously Resistance Day). After the war, independence from the British was negotiated by the nationalists. However, General Aung San and other cabinet ministers were assassinated on 19th July 1948, now commemorated as Martyrs' Day. Independence was eventually won on 4th January 1948.

Protest and Insurrection

The insurrections and protests which broke out in Burma shortly after independence have in fact continued to the present day.

Up to the late 1950s the political and economic situation was unstable and in 1958 a *coup d'etat* by the armed forces brought a caretaker government into power. Elections were held in 1960 to return power to civil rule. However, insurrection became more severe with the Shan still claiming the right to secession which had been promised them in the Panglong Agreement of 1947.

Another *coup d'etat* in March 1962 brought the Revolutionary Council to power and, soon after, the government declared its socialist aims under policies known as The Burmese Way to Socialism. The Burma Socialist Party was also officially formed, but the government's extreme isolationism and attempts to be self-sufficient caused severe economic repercussions. Protest manifested itself in terms of frequent student demonstrations and workers' strikes.

In 1988 this protest reached a head when a student brawl in a tea shop sparked nationwide demonstrations. These were brutally suppressed by a military coup and the State Law and Order Restoration Council (SLORC) formed a government. The country's name was changed from the Socialist Republic of Burma to the Union of Myanmar and the names of towns and roads were all changed to Burmese. Rangoon symbolically became Yangon, meaning "end of strife".

By the time elections were held in May of 1990, more than 200 political parties had been formed under proposals for a multi-party form of government. The largest of these, the National League for Democracy (NLD), was headed by Daw Aung San Suu Kyi, daughter of General Aung San. Her party won the elections by a landslide, despite the fact that she herself was placed under house arrest in July 1989, after continuous harassment during her travels throughout the country giving talks and meeting people. She was awarded the Nobel Peace Prize in 1991 but, along with many of her supporters, continues to remain under arrest, refusing to accept exile.

Burma's human rights record remains poor in international terms even though future economic aid and foreign investments appear to hinge on this issue.

Key Dates

849   Founding of Pagan.

1044   Anawrahta becomes King of Pagan and forms the first Burmese Empire. Buddhism is brought to Burma.

1287   Kublai Khan and his Mongol army destroy Pagan. Burma disintegrates into small states for the next three centuries.

1551   Bayinnaung reconquers former territories and founds the second Burmese Empire. After his death in 1581 the country slowly falls apart.

1755   Alaungpaya of Shwebo reunites the country and forms the third Burmese Empire.

1824   The first Anglo-Burmese War breaks out and Arakan and Tenasserim are ceded to the British.

1852   The second Anglo-Burmese War results in the loss of lower Burma to the British.

1886   The third Anglo-Burmese War makes Burma a province of British India and the Burmese royal family is exiled to India.

1906   The Young Men's Buddhist Association (YMBA) is formed. This association became an important nationalist organisation.

1937   Burma separates from India with a new constitution and legislative council.

1943   Burma falls under Japanese occupation.

1945   27th March, General Aung San leads open resistance to the Japanese.

       5th May, the British reoccupy Rangoon.

1947   1st January, Aung San leads á delegation to London to negotiate independence.

       12th February, the Panglong Agreement is signed by representatives of Kachin, Kayah, Karen, Chin, Shan and other ethnic groups.

       19th July, Aung San and his cabinet are assassinated. Prime Minister U Nu forms a new cabinet.

1948   4th January, Burma gains independence and becomes the Union of Burma. Insurgencies break out soon after.

1949   The Karen army reaches the outskirts of Rangoon but the government regain control.

1951   Elections are held. The economy declines, suffering from the fall in the world price of rice.

1958   A caretaker government steps in as the main political party.

1960   Elections are held but insurrection becomes more severe as the Shan claim secession.

1962   The Revolutionary Council takes over.

1964   Nationalisation of private trading firms, banks, industries, schools and hospitals is carried out, along with demonetisation.

1974   A new constitution is adopted and Burma follows the Burmese Way to Socialism, a policy of self-reliance, isolation and strict neutrality.

1985   Demonetisation of K100 and K500 notes with limited compensation after one year.

1987   Demonetisation of K25 and K75 notes without compensation.

1988   18th September, student-led demonstrations sparked by demonetisation lead to a military coup. The SLORC forms local governing bodies at all levels of administration.

1989   Burma becomes the Union of Myanmar.

1990   In May, elections are held. The NLD, headed by Aung San Suu Kyi, wins by a landslide.

1993   The National Convention for drawing up the nation's new constitution convenes.

ECONOMY

Burma's economy remains largely agricultural, despite efforts to build a strong manufacturing sector. Manufacturing is still very outdated and industries are mainly state-owned. The lack of new technology, shortage of spare parts and scarcity of raw materials are the result of the lack of foreign exchange, which is in turn caused by low exports. An economic vicious circle is clearly in operation in Burma.

However, Burma's natural resources have always been described as abundant. The country possesses forests of teak, hardwoods and bamboo; precious gems such as rubies, sapphires and jade; mineral resources of silver, lead, tungsten and marble; and natural gas and oil. Apart from the British Oil Company's development in the Yenangyaung area during colonial times, Burma's gas and oil resources (particularly offshore) remain largely untapped. Miles of beautiful and unpolluted beaches are also largely undeveloped due to a lack of security and capital.

Consequently Burma remains an agricultural country, with 40 per cent of its economy based on farming. The major industrial crops are rice, beans and pulses, cotton, tobacco, jute, sugar cane, rubber and coconut. Fish and shrimp are also abundant in Burma's waters, and poachers frequently enter from neighbouring countries to fish.

As far as export revenues are concerned, teak and hardwood exports have overtaken Burma's traditional rice economy in recent years. Beans and pulses are also a major export, as are minerals and precious gems. Since the normalisation of border trade, revenues which had formerly been lost to the black market have been regained somewhat.

In opening up the economy, the role of the private sector still appears ambiguous. Government control has by no means been relinquished and the state sector, with its large unprofitable industries, still needs to be tackled. Much-needed foreign investment is likely to remain lacking until Burma's political situation can be resolved.

Money

The monetary unit in Burma is the *kyat* (pronounced "chat" and abbreviated as K). It is made up of 100 *pyas*. *Kyat* come in denominations of 1, 5, 10, 45, 90 and 200. Coins are seldom seen as inflation is so high that they are no longer effective. In fact it is rumoured that coins are melted down so that the metal may be used.

Demonetisation, whereby legal tender is declared unusable, has been carried out no less than three times in the past thirty years in Burma. Those with any savings found that they were worthless overnight and they were rarely given compensation. The political and economic reason behind this demonetisation was to hit at black market traders who held large amounts of currency outside the banking system. In the process, however, it also hit everyday people, especially the working class and retired.

The confidence in the national currency remains low today. People still do not wish to use the banks and either hold currency at home or buy gold, jewellery and real estate to diversify their savings. Where money is concerned, the man on the street is now reluctant to place all his eggs in one basket.

For visitors to Burma, banks issue Foreign Exchange Certificates (F.E.C.) like those in operation in China.

Effects on Everyday Life

The effect of economic instability on everyday life has been hard on the Burmese. The older generation in particular have lived through times of relative prosperity and economic growth, only to experience the very real financial loss of overnight demonetisation and a scarcity of basic foods and services which were once readily available.

The distribution of income is very uneven in Burma, although, to help overcome hardship, a secondary distribution often goes on. This takes the form of charitable feasts and donations. For example, if a villager wins a lottery prize or increases his income from a good harvest, he may hold a *shinbyu* ceremony during which he will give a feast for fellow villagers if he can afford it (see Chapter Two). Wealthier members of the community will be sure to invite the whole village and in this way many mouths are fed.

In addition, the difficulty of obtaining basic goods and services has forced the Burmese to develop their own brand of "recycling". The objective behind this is hardly ecological; it is actually scarcity that forces people to make use of literally everything and does not allow them the luxury of throwing anything away. Such items as empty bottles, chocolate boxes, old shoes and clothes, mattresses and pillows, bed sheets, books and newspapers all are hoarded for some future use. For instance, old tyres may be made into slippers, or newspapers and old office stationery can be sold to make paper bags and wrapping paper.

This practice may also be due to the fact that plastic has not become the ubiquitous article that it has elsewhere in the world. Leaves are still used to wrap many articles of food and, in place of string, various types of fibre or twine are used. These biodegradable articles can help to keep the environment clean but there is no strong sense of cleanliness amongst the Burmese, who tend to drop litter everywhere. The use of leaves and vines is sure to deplete supplies and, as with many natural resources in Burma, there is no systematic replenishing and cultivation, just a continuous harvesting.

LITERACY

The Burmese are highly literate. The official literacy estimate set the figure at 82 per cent of the population and, in fact, Burma won a UNESCO award for its effective literacy campaign in the early 1970s. However, because the government wanted the country to receive Least Developed Status in order to get relief for its national debt, the "effective" literacy rate was quoted as being much lower.

The population is largely literate because of the traditional system of monastic learning where boys and girls would go to the local monastery to be taught the three R's. In return they would sweep the compound, fetch water and perform other errands and duties for the monks.

Children on their way to school across Inle Lake.

Modern schooling in Burma usually consists of two years of pre-school, four of primary and four of middle. High school is two years and most university courses are four. Children begin school at about four or five but many only continue to the fourth grade or "standard" (aged around ten). This is particularly so in rural areas where parents need their children to help with farming activities and usually feel that primary education is quite adequate.

Those who can, try to make it to university as degrees are prestigious and coveted awards. In fact, in Burma, the more letters one has after one's name the better. This seems to apply whatever the qualification, a common suffix being E.T.E.C., meaning Electrical Training Evening Classes!

University education has seen a good deal of reorganisation in recent years, breaking up the larger and older institutions into smaller organisations. This was largely meant to separate the student population into smaller groups to deter future unrest and protesting.

Monks on their way to a feast ceremony, during which they will chant prayers and transfer merit to all beings.

Chapter Two

A LIFETIME OF CEREMONY

Burmese lifecycle ceremonies, or rites of passage, are classified into *tha yei* and *na yei*. *Tha yei* stands for the happy occasions and *na yei* for the sad ones. The former includes births, marriages, birthdays and engagements, while the latter includes sickness and death.

The Burmese love ceremony and, if they can possibly afford it, they try to have elaborate celebrations to which they can invite all their family, friends and neighbours. Even if they cannot afford this they are often willing to get into substantial debt in order to celebrate in style. A great amount of time, money and energy is expended planning ceremonies and celebrations in Burma, but helpers are always plentiful on these occasions and relatives are expected to do their family duty by getting involved in whatever way they can.

BIRTHS

From the time a couple get married they are continually asked when the first child will be arriving! It is considered very odd for a couple not to want to have any children and all parents are eager to become grandparents. Barren couples are always pitied. In rural areas this attitude may stem from the fact that people do not mind having many children because of the high infant mortality rates, the use of child labour and for security in old age.

As soon as the wife is expecting there is excitement in the family. Preparations are made, but there are many superstitions surrounding childbirth which still has high mortality rates for both mother and child. For instance, as disposable diapers have not yet reached Burma, expectant mothers will prepare a stock of cloth that can be used. These are sewn but not completely finished off. It's the same with baby clothes, where hems are left unfinished. The superstition is that to be over-prepared will bring misfortune on the new baby. If clothes are bought they are not kept with the mother-to-be but with some other person who will bring them over only after the baby is born.

Pregnant ladies also have to be careful about what they eat. There are taboos about eating too much chilli, bananas and glutinous rice, and about not going to funerals or visiting cemeteries. They will often not be invited to weddings and, even if invited, may not wish to go. Alternatively, the wedding couple will be asked if they mind a pregnant guest attending. However, educated Burmese do not pay too much attention to these superstitions.

Gifts

Once a friend or colleague has a new baby it is usual to give a small gift, such as pieces of cloth, baby clothes, feeding bottles, talcum powder and so on. Close friends try to visit the mother and baby in the hospital. Friends visiting from afar will not only bring presents, but will often be given them in return when they leave.

If you are going to be away when your friend or colleague gives birth and you wish to give a present anyway, it is a good idea to give the gift to a close friend of the mother-to-be who will give it on your behalf when the time comes. Do not give it earlier because many women are still quite superstitious when it comes to childbirth and would rather not take chances.

Feasts

It is usual for the baby's arrival to be celebrated with a naming day feast or "100 days old" feast. Monks are invited over for an early morning or mid-morning meal, prayers will be chanted and then the guests will be fed. (See Chapter Five for more on feasts.)

CHILDHOOD

Burmese children are very much indulged and spoilt. You may find that your domestic staff tend to do this with your own children. However, you should never express admiration of children because Burmese believe that evil spirits will hear and harm them. Never say how fat a baby or child is, or how chubby or heavy.

One of the most important occasions in a boy's life is the *shinbyu* ceremony when, for a short period, he becomes a novice in the local Buddhist monastery. This can be from a few days to a week or more. Parents and grandparents are very proud and happy on this occasion as they receive great merit from the novitiation. At this time they also have a chance to offer robes, food and money to the monks, as well as a feast for guests. In rural areas, many parents go into debt in order to provide a grand feast.

For girls, ear-piercing ceremonies used to be a ritual occasion but they are not widely celebrated now. However, girls can also have a novitiation ceremony if they become nuns in a local nunnery.

Feasts for monks are given for both the *shinbyu* and when girls

The novitiation of young Burmese boys is a happy occasion.

enter a nunnery. For the ear-piercing ceremony, a feast for monks and guests is also the norm. If you are invited, there is no need to bring a gift. Your presence at the ceremony or the feast is all that is required.

These ceremonies are very colourful as the participants will be dressed in traditional costume. Wealthier hosts may even hire professional dancers and entertainers. It is usual to take photographs on these occasions and many of the guests will gladly pose if you wish to do so.

ENGAGEMENTS

Couples who have had long and happy marriages are the preferred guests at an engagement party. Widows, widowers and divorcees are never invited to be guests of honour.

Both families will usually have at least one couple as guests of honour and the male guest of honour has to make a speech about the qualities and qualifications of the prospective bridegroom. Then, on behalf of the latter's parents, he formally requests the hand of the bride-to-be.

These engagement parties are small affairs, with only close friends and relatives invited. If a more formal affair is planned, it will often be held in a small suite at a hotel, with as many as 50 guests. Light refreshments will be provided.

Gifts are not necessary on these occasions.

Among Christians, engagements are also celebrated with an exchange of rings.

WEDDINGS

Weddings among the Burmese do not have religious significance and couples are not married by monks. According to Burmese Buddhist law, if a man and woman are recognised as a couple by seven houses to the right and seven houses to the left of their home, then they can become husband and wife. They can be married in a ceremony conducted by any distinguished couple, including government ministers, chief justices, barristers and professors. Again, however, the couple performing the ceremony should be one with a long and happy marriage, preferably blessed with many children. If this is not possible or convenient, the bride and groom will simply visit a registry of marriages and sign a marriage certificate. Christian marriages are solemnised in churches, as in other Christian communities.

Large formal weddings are held at hotels and guests can number 500 or more. The Burmese concept of "face" (see Chapter Three) requires that no one who ought to be invited is left out.

Coffee and tea are served at wedding parties, as well as tea-time food like sandwiches, cakes, meat puffs and ice-cream. This type of fare has been served for years, since the time the hotels were run by foreign firms. The menu has only seen a change in quality as ingredients were exchanged for low-quality ones, the finer foods and goods being sold on the black market by those who pilfered them. It seems that at weddings no one has ever bothered to serve anything

A formal wedding allows everyone to wear their best clothes and jewellery.

else. At The Strand Hotel you may be served butter rice and chicken curry, but many still seem to prefer tea, cakes and sandwiches for wedding receptions.

Being able to have a wedding at a big hotel is a status symbol, the ability to invite guests in their hundreds being proof of one's wealth and hospitality.

You are likely to witness at least one of these weddings in a hotel and can have a chance to photograph the brightly coloured traditional clothes worn by the bride and groom. The guests will also be wearing their best clothes and the women their loveliest jewellery. All of it is real as costume jewellery is hardly ever worn on these occasions. This is the time to show off one's wealth and acquisitions.

Weddings are not celebrated during the months of Buddhist Lent which roughly fall between June and September.

Gifts

For weddings, cash is given only when it appears that the bridal couple are in somewhat needy circumstances, for example when both bride and groom are still students in college or when they do not yet have established jobs. Cash gifts in multiples of one hundred are commonly given since a hundred is a symbol of long life and, by inference, a long marriage. One would give cash gifts to one's domestic staff, to employees or junior clerical officers.

Otherwise, household items like bed linen, towels, crockery, cutlery, kitchenware, tableware and appliances are acceptable gifts. Pieces of cloth for the bride to make clothes are sometimes given. Photo albums are also useful presents since many photos are taken and viewed by all guests and visitors later on.

Some superstitions exist about giving knives and scissors as gifts, so it's better not to do so. Gifts which are black in colour should also be avoided.

Decorative items should be considered only where utilitarian gifts have been exhausted. In Burma it is functional items which are needed more. Extremely luxurious gifts may not be meaningful if their use is somewhat limited. For example, a fine handmade doll may not be significantly appreciated because a lot of things in Burma are hand-made anyway.

In offices, funds are pooled to buy a more sumptuous gift for the wedding couple. The names of all the givers are signed on the card. This method is easy on the pockets of office workers who do not earn much. Sometimes a sliding scale is arranged whereby the head of the office contributes the most and the juniors the least. If you wish to participate in such a collection you should make your wishes clear, otherwise it will be assumed that you will be giving a present individually.

Superstitions and Beliefs

Astrological calculations are made for all important matters in Bur-mese life, from choosing business partners to dates for laying the foundations of important buildings.

Not surprisingly, then, the Burmese will often consult astrologers or psychics about all aspects of married life. This includes the choice of a partner, the most auspicious day for the wedding and what to do to make the marriage a long and successful one.

Choosing names for children, companies and brands is also astrologically calculated, the logic here being that is better to be safe than sorry. Of course if everything were to depend on astrology we would all be millionaires by now! (See Chapter Three for more on superstitions.)

SICKNESS

When someone is seriously ill and in hospital the fact is made known to those closest to that person. If he or she is very ill it is important to make a call at the hospital if you can. *Na yei* are given more weight than happy events as far as attendance and effort is concerned.

Unlike Westerners, who would prefer not to have callers during a hospitalisation, the Burmese will arrive in their dozens, taking turns to go up and see the patient. Even colleagues, superiors and juniors, will make an effort to visit.

Hospitalisation for locals is a difficult and costly business. As nurses are expensive and in demand, it often requires a good deal of organisation as to who will be the patient's attendant for the day and for the night. In addition to that, food must be sent for as hospitals have not provided meals since the late 1960s. In the provinces, cartloads of relatives from a village will camp in the hospital compound, cook over a log fire and take care of the patient! Such camps may stay *in situ* for quite some time, depending on the illness of the patient.

In Burma, old people are treated with respect and loving care if younger people can possibly give it. Filial duty is emphasised and is believed to bring many blessings. However, many old people are afraid of hospitals and do not wish to be hospitalised if they can help it. Hospitals are perceived as places where one is inevitably sent to die. There may have been some truth in this in the old days when people only went to hospitals if it was nearly too late and deaths soon after hospitalisation were frequent.

(For ideas on appropriate things to bring when you visit a sick friend, see Chapter Four.)

DEATH

Death is classified with *na yei* (sad ceremonies). To the Burmese, death is just one stage in the cycle of life and for this reason there are no official mourning periods specified by religion. Families and friends will grieve, but they should not do so for long periods of time.

When a person dies at home the body is bathed and clothed in that person's favourite or newest clothing. They are then laid out on a bed decorated with lace, netting and flowers. Afterwards the bed is often donated to the local monastery as a gesture of goodwill which will help the dead along the cycle of life. On the day of death a monk will be invited over for a meal and will offer prayers for the dead.

If a person dies in hospital or away from home, the body is not allowed back into the perimeters of the village or street where the deceased lived. It will be kept at the morgue, although in rural areas it is not uncommon to see a coffin with its corpse laid out for burial on the outskirts of the village.

As soon as a death occurs it is made known to all family and friends who must make every effort to help the bereaved family in any way they can. This includes cooking, caring for the children, entertaining callers throughout the day (and frequently the night) and keeping vigil until the seventh day when the wake is over. On this last day a feast is again given to monks and offerings are made. Through this act of merit (called *dana*) the deceased's spirit may go peacefully on to its next existence.

At a Wake

As it is believed that the spirit of the dead remains near the body or home for up to a week after death, a wake is held for most of this period. However, in cases where death occurs just before Burmese New Year the funeral will be held as quickly as possible so that it will not be carried over into the new year and bring bad luck.

When a person dies there will usually be a large canvas tent-like structure in front of the house. The body of the deceased may lie there or at the mortuary, but callers will still visit their home and family. During the wake the house doors are left open and friends and relatives must keep vigil in turn during the nights. There will be endless pots of tea and card games to keep them awake.

When you visit during the day, Burmese tea and black melon seeds are served while you pay your respects and talk to the deceased's family. There is no need to talk much. It is your presence that is appreciated. There is also no need to say goodbye. You can just quietly leave and ask any other relative around to tell the bereaved that you are going.

Funerals

Funerals usually take place on the third or fifth day after death. Burial is the norm in Burma, although in Rangoon cremation is more common. The ceremony usually includes the recitation of prayers by visiting monks and an official notice read by the deceased's employers, releasing the dead from his or her duties.

Funerals require attendance and you may be surprised at the number of working hours lost in attending them. For close kin especially, attendance is so important that usually everything is dropped as soon as the news is received.

One may be forgiven for not attending a wedding but to fail in showing your face at a funeral means that you have no regard for the deceased and their family. If you are informed of the death of a friend or acquaintance, a telegram, letter or card must be sent if you cannot go personally. The fact that you are on the list of those to be informed means that you are being given a chance not to lose face by not attending the funeral or visiting the home of the deceased. Many are seriously offended if they did not know of the death of someone in time to attend the funeral or to show their respect in other ways.

When bitter quarrels arise between friends and relatives in Burma, they may curse one another with the oath, "Don't come to my funeral when I die!" Only the deepest and most unforgiving hatred brings out this exclamation, which shows how much the Burmese value attendance at funerals.

When a colleague passes away, all office staff will attend the funeral. They help in many ways, either by cash contributions, donating paper fans, prayer books and pamphlets, or providing buses to carry mourners. Office work may slow down or even stop as these social obligations are very important to office staff. Only the most serious circumstances or plans are considered excuse enough for not showing one's face at a funeral.

What to Do and Wear

Your presence at the home of the deceased will be very much appreciated in itself.

Gifts of money are valued if the family are in a lower income bracket. One may give flowers, but they do not really have much significance in Burma. When you cannot attend, a card, telegram or letter of condolence will be sufficient.

Do not wear bright colours. Wear navy, black or something sober, even though the Burmese do not have an official mourning colour. Shorts and short skirts should, of course, be avoided.

Do not greet the bereaved family with the Burmese greeting *mingala-ba* which means "auspiciousness to you". Death is not an auspicious occasion.

FESTIVALS

The Burmese have a festival for every month in their calendar. This calendar, traditionally consists of twelve lunar months. As lunar months differ from solar months in the number of days, an extra month, known as a "second Waso month" is added every few years, a bit like a leap year. The Burmese year 1355 begins in April 1993 and ends in mid-April 1994. However, for religious matters the Burmese use the Buddhist calendar. This is also the lunar calendar, but the calculations begin from the year of Buddha's Enlightenment. Thus, 1993 is 2536-2537 according to Buddhist Era.

Calendar of Festivals

Festival	Burmese Month	English Month
Water Festival	Tagu	March–April
Kasone Banyan-Watering	Kasone	April–May
Sar-pyan-pwe*	Nayone	May–June
Waso Robe Offering	Waso	June–July
Sar-yay-dan-me-pwe*	Wagaung	July–August

Festival crowd.

Boat Festival	Tawthalin	August–September
Festival of Lights	Thadingyut	September–October
Kahtein Robe Offering	Tazaungmone	October–November
*Sar-so-daw-pwe**	Nadaw	November–December
Equestrian Festival	Pyatho	December–January
Hta-mane Festival	Tabodwei	January–February
Sand Pagoda Festival	Tabaung	February–March

Sar-pyan-pwe is the time when monks take their examinations in the Buddhist scriptures. *Sar-yay-dan-me-pwe* is a festival in which lots are drawn lots for a Buddha image prize. *Sar-so-daw-pwe* celebrates the poets and literary figures of Burma.

Holidays

Burma has a considerable number of holidays to celebrate festivals and to commemorate heroes and national events.

Jan 4	Independence Day; when independence from the British was attained.
Feb 12	Union Day; when the Panglong Agreement of 1947 was signed between the Burmese and leaders of the major ethnic groups, aiming towards a Union of Burma.
Mar 2	Originally the day of the 1962 *coup d'etat* by the Revolutionary Council, now celebrated as Peasants Day.
Mar 27	Tatmadaw Day (Armed Forces Day); celebrates the day when the Burmese army marched against the Japanese.
April	Water festival.
May 1	Workers' Day (the Burmese equivalent of Labour Day).
May	Kasone Banyan-Watering Festival.
Jul 19	Martyrs' Day; when Aung San and other cabinet ministers were assassinated.

Dec	National Day; this falls on the tenth waning moon day of Tazaungmone.
Dec	Karen New Year; this falls on the first waxing moon day of Pyatho.
Dec 25	Christmas Day.

Because of the number of public holidays, it is not a custom to extend the holiday to Monday should it fall on a Sunday. (Government departments are closed on Saturdays and Sundays.)

Water Festival

The water festival in April lasts three to five days, although this can be extended to a week if the holiday falls over a weekend. The water festival welcomes in the Burmese New Year. Business slows down or practically stops at this time of year, so it is not a good idea to plan business trips then.

This festival (similar to Songkran in Thailand) is eagerly awaited by young people and children. For teenagers, especially, it is a time to see and be seen, to mix with people their own age in a holiday environment. Known as *Thin gyan* or *Tha gyan* (*gy* is equivalent to "j"), the festival is often prepared for several months in advance, with songs, dances and skits being rehearsed, and stages being designed or set up.

But, of course, the focus of the whole festival is water. Symbolically the sprinkling of water washes away the sins and bad luck of the old year in preparation for the new, although in reality the practice becomes an excuse for endless practical jokes where whole barrels or even hose pipes of water are directed at friends, relatives and anyone else who gets in the way.

Special marquees called *pandal* (derived from Tamil word *pendel*) are set up on roadsides, along with stages for dances and songs. The *pandal* may belong to each quarter of the town, to a group of friends, families or associations, or to government departments or companies who collect the money and organise the whole show. Rows of water barrels line the front of the *pandal* and girls take turns to throw water at truck-loads of people driving from one *pandal* to another just for the purpose of getting soaked.

The water festival may thus be experienced either as one of the assailants throwing water from one of the *pandal* or as part of the group of targets in the vehicles. It is all great fun and no one is supposed to get angry, even when a complete stranger shouts insults at you on the street or drenches you while passing by. Lots of teasing goes on, some of which may end up in fights, especially as many young people get well and truly drunk, thus having less control over what they do and say.

Accidents are quite common and, as a participant, one should not only be careful of getting hurt from very rough water throwing, but should be wary of pickpockets in the crowd. A watchful eye should especially be kept on children and eyes and ears should be well covered with thick towels to avoid injury. Eardrums have been known to be pierced by water being sprayed at high pressure. Drivers must also be aware of the danger caused by wet streets, as traffic accidents are common at this time.

Older people will rarely participate in these vigorous activities and generally prefer to stay at home or keep the Eight Precepts (see Glossary) by visiting monasteries or meditation centres. Others may go for a long holiday, having seen enough of water festivals over the years.

Visitors to Burma, however, should really experience the fun of this colourful festival at least once. The diplomatic corps are usually treated to a special water festival celebration arranged by the Ministry of Foreign Affairs, which comes complete with dances, food and visits to town for water throwing.

What to Wear

It is best to wear thick clothes, preferably denim shirts and jeans which take the sting away from the splashes of water, commonly thrown out of small condensed milk tins. Do not wear white or thin materials, or colours which will run, as every item of clothing is sure to cling to you the wetter you get. Burmese girls are often seen walking home sopping wet with the hem of their sarong in tatters. Unfortunately, at this time of year traditional Burmese ladieswear is not as comfortable or convenient as it usually is: try walking in a completely wet sarong – it's just like having a wet bandage wrapped around your legs. At least Burmese men can wear trousers, but most of the women still prefer traditional dress.

If you intend actively participating in the festival it's a good idea to take a change of clothing and underwear in a waterproof bag, along with an extra towel. Water throwers try to get rid of grievances and aggression at this time and they can be quite indiscriminate in their aim.

Kasone Banyan-Watering

It was on the full moon day of Kasone that the Buddha was born, attained Enlightenment and finally passed away. His Enlightenment occurred as he sat under a banyan tree and thus one will find such trees planted in almost every pagoda and monastery in Burma. The tree is sacred amongst Buddhists and banyan tree-watering ceremonies are conducted.

Such a watering ceremony can be seen at the Shwe Dagon, the Sule and other pagodas and monasteries. Young girls will carry earthen water pots filled with water and take turns to water the banyan tree, the base of which is often enclosed in a decorative concrete structure.

Waso Robe-Offering

The day of the full moon in the month of Waso marks the beginning of Lent, which spans the three months of the rainy season. It commemorates the preaching of Buddha's first sermon, 49 days after his

Enlightenment. Buddhists observe this day by keeping the Eight Precepts. Monks will be offered meals by disciples and sermons are delivered. A robe-offering ceremony is also performed not later than the full-moon day of Waso as, after this day, the monks are forbidden to travel and are required to spend Lent in the monasteries. The robes are offered to them for use during this period of retreat.

Festival of Lights (Thadingyut)

This festival is held at the end of Lent on the full moon day of Thadingyut. It celebrates the descent of the Buddha from heaven after he preached the *Abidhamma* (the most difficult of Buddhist teachings) to his mother who was reborn in heaven.

On or around the festival day it is a custom to pay respects to elders by offering presents of fruit, cake or *longyi* (lengths of cloth worn as a sarong). Elders include grandparents, uncles, aunts, teachers, professors, and lecturers.

Every house is lit up at night, either with strings of electric lights, candles or paper lanterns. Electricity being rather unpredictable, most families now just use candles and even then just a token few are lighted as candles are also rather expensive.

The lights all over the towns look lovely and government offices often try to outdo each other in designing the decorations. Various streets in the major towns are also lit up and closed off to traffic. Food and handicraft stalls are lined up on the roadsides and Burmese shows of dancing and drama (known as *pwes*) are staged at one end of the main street.

If you are going to look at or join in the festivities, again beware of pickpockets who are always rife at festival times in Burma. Try not to take your passport and valuables with you as the streets become very crowded. It is good to go along with some Burmese friends who are aware of the dangers.

Kahtein Robe-Offering

The Kahtein robe-offering is performed during the month of Tazaungmone. Robes and other articles are offered to monks and feasts are held.

A second festival of lights, called *Tazaungdaing*, is celebrated at this time, about a month after the first one. It is very similar to the first festival except that different parts of the towns and cities may be lit up.

During this festival, the Shwe Dagon Pagoda in Rangoon has an all-night robe-weaving contest. The robes must be finished by dawn when they are offered to the Buddha images in the pagoda. Similar robe-weaving contests take place around the country, but this is the most famous. Large crowds are attracted to the spectacle and, as there are usually not enough security people around, you should keep an eye on your valuables.

At this time practical jokes are frequently played on neighbours and family: moving the flower pots or washing line about and hiding things are common jokes.

Hta-ma-ne *Festival (Tabodwei Full Moon)*

This festival celebrates a good harvest, although the name actually comes from the food traditionally eaten at this time.

Hta-ma-ne is a savoury concoction made of glutinous rice cooked with groundnuts, coconut shreds, sesame oil, ginger and garlic. Grown men are usually needed to make the mixture as it is very thick and hard to stir. They make it in huge pans over open fires in gardens or monasteries. Because of the quantity they are often seen stirring it with what look like paddles or oars. Later, packets of the gooey *hta-ma-ne,* wrapped in banana leaves, are distributed to neighbours.

Monasteries also prepare *hta-ma-ne* with the chief abbot supervising and then distributing the packets to disciples.

Pagoda Festivals (Hpaya Pwe)

Being a land of pagodas, all the important ones in the land have their own festival days, which fall on various full moon days of the Burmese calendar.

The most famous, the Shwe Dagon in Rangoon, celebrates its festival in the month of Tabaung which falls in February and March. The festival is held in the grounds of the pagoda at the foot of the hill on which it stands. Many stalls are set up here, selling food, handicrafts, textiles and other local products. Ferris wheels and merry-go-rounds are there for the children. Large structures of bamboo-matting are erected where Burmese songs, dances and plays, usually from the *Jataka* (stories of Buddha's life), are performed by famous Burmese dance troupes. Villagers from the provinces around Rangoon will come to spend the night watching the shows, eating their favourite delicacies and going home in their bullock carts only in the morning

However, if you are intending to visit one of these festivals, you should be warned that there is a real fire hazard because of the unmanaged crowds and the flammable nature of most of the structures erected for the celebrations.

Ethnic Festivals

Each of the ethnic groups in Burma has its own festivals, the most famous of which are the Karen New Year, Kachin Manao Festival and Pao Rocket-Firing Festivals. However, it may be difficult for the visitor to get to see them as even locals from the valleys find it hard to reach the mountain areas.

The Karen New Year is a national holiday and is celebrated by the Karen with dances and songs. Dances are performed by groups and rehearsals start months earlier. The Karen dress in their ethnic costume of tunics and beautiful woven *longyi* (usually red with colourful stripes). The women tie coloured scarves in their hair. If you live in Rangoon, there are dances at Insein, a suburb in northwest Rangoon where the Karen communities are concentrated. The Karen state capital, Pa-an, holds the grandest celebrations at this time.

Among the festivals being revived by the current government is the ancient Boat Festival which is celebrated on the Royal Lakes and has traditional boats being rowed by boatsmen in traditional costume. Another is the Equestrian Festival, featuring shows of military skills on horseback.

Nat Pwe

While the Burmese are Buddhists, many still cling to their older animistic roots. This takes the form of worshipping spirits, called *nat*, to whom prayers and offerings are made at a small shrine in the home. Such spirit worship is prevalent in the Upper Burma regions and amongst the many ethnic groups.

Taungbyon, about 13 miles north of Mandalay, is the location of the Taungbyon *Nat Pwe* (or Spirit Festival), the most famous animist celebration. This takes place in August when train-loads of worshippers arrive to pray to the powerful spirits of the two Taungbyon brothers, executed by the king in the 11th century.

Burmese *nat* worshippers may pray to some or all of the pantheon of 37 *nat*, most of whom died violent deaths before becoming spirits.

Worship is generally based on fear of being harmed or punished by the *nat*, and the hope that favours will be bestowed in return for prayers.

Nat pwe can also be seen in Rangoon, where crowds of people may gather inside bamboo *pandals* for music and dancing. There are special songs for the *nat* and mediums may become possessed by the spirits to dance or talk.

Christmas

Christmas in Burma is celebrated by Christians just as it is in other parts of the world, with church services, carol singing, small parties and gift giving. The ethnic groups have prominent Christian communities and there are also Burmese Christians. Carol singing is especially popular amongst the very musical Karen groups.

Incidentally, those who expect a longish holiday season from Christmas to New Year should be warned that there isn't one in Burma. New Year's Day is not a public holiday.

ADVICE ON GIFT GIVING

You may be surprised to hear protests when you give someone a gift. They say, "You shouldn't have bothered," or "You shouldn't have gone to so much trouble." These protests are sincerely meant. The Burmese genuinely feel that, in friendship, it is not important whether you give presents or not.

Your gift will probably not be opened in your presence unless you ask your friend to do so. The reason is to avoid appearing avaricious. Similarly, once your present has been opened you may not hear effusive words of appreciation. Your friend is here suffering from that national feeling called *ah-nar-de* (see Chapter Three) which places him in a dilemma: to accept your gift too readily would appear greedy, but not to accept it would be equally rude.

He may not let on whether the gift you give is to his liking or not but, underneath, he will be grateful that you have given him something and that he has not been forgotten.

Do not be disappointed by what seems like a lack of appreciation and don't worry that the gift was not a good choice: it will always be considered valuable in some way. He can resell it to get something he really needs if he cannot use it himself. While you may be hurt by this, you must remember the economic situation in Burma. In the long run it is surely best for a friend to get what he needs rather than what he doesn't. (See Chapter Five for more information on gifts.)

Chapter Three

BURMESE PERCEPTIONS

It has frequently been said that being Burmese is synonymous with being Buddhist. This may seem a simplistic definition, but it is true that the great majority of Burmese are Buddhists and that they tend to think of their identity in terms of religion first.

There are two main streams of Buddhism: Mahayana and Theravada (sometimes called Hinayana). Mahayana Buddhism is mainly found in Tibet, China, Japan and Korea, while the latter is practised in Sri Lanka, Thailand, Burma, Cambodia and Laos. The Burmese clearly show a preference for other Theravada Buddhists and Burma is well-known for its important centres of learning for scripture and meditation within this tradition.

Converts to Buddhism are greatly admired, although there is never a strong push towards conversion as there is in some religions. A popular magazine on Buddhism carries an article every month on converts of various nationalities and gives their reasons for coming to Burma as yogis.

Kan

Burmese believe in the Buddhist concept of *kan,* or karma, according to which good begets good and evil begets evil. Every thought, word or act is believed to have an effect on one's karma, which literally means "intention". So it is not simply what we do that influences our lives, but also our intentions behind the deed. (Refined definitions of the different kinds of karma can be found in most books on Buddhism.)

Typical offerings of flowers and leaves at a small Buddhist shrine.

55

The belief in *kan* is said to be the root of poverty in Burma by a number of economic and social analysts. This may be because it is a belief which makes help ineffectual in the long term and proves frustrating to those who would like to teach the poor in Burma to help themselves.

Belief in *kan* is usually labelled a fatalistic attitude towards life, since everything that happens is said to be caused by our actions in a past life which is now beyond our control. Disasters, catastrophes and sudden deaths are all brought about by karma and are therefore accepted. Actually this is only a layman's perception of karma. Buddhists believe that while one cannot change one's past, it is possible to change the future. In this sense, belief in karma is positive and should not be held responsible for poverty or a lack of positive action to improve the quality of life in Burma.

Merits (Kutho) *and Defilements* (Akutho)

Urging others to do good deeds on the grounds that merit (*kutho*) will accrue is very common and most people are willing to go along with such persuasion. For example, when donations for charity are collected, the donor is often reminded of the merits of *dana* and being charitable (*dana* is the Pali word for "giving" or "charity").

Being filial is also part of gaining good merit, as parents (together with teachers) are ranked just after the Triple Gems in order of respect. The Triple Gems comprise the Buddha, the *Dhamma* (his teachings) and the *Sangha* (his disciples the monks). Looking after one's parents is supposed to give great merit, one of them being that such a son or daughter will never become poor.

Together with the belief in karma is the belief in cycles and planes of existence. According to Buddhist philosophy, all living things are believed to go through endless cycles of existence, known as *than-tha-yar* (existence itself is known as *ba wa* in Burmese). Additionally, they move through various planes of existence, of which there are 31. These planes are the lower planes (including hell, animals and ghosts), the human plane and the higher planes of celestial existence.

Nirvana is the goal of any devout Buddhist who wishes to be freed from the cycle of existence. Charity (*dana*), morality (*sila*) and insight or wisdom (*bhavana*) are the three requirements of the journey to *Nirvana*. Charity is the most easily accomplished of these, but the Five Precepts of *sila*, namely abstention from killing living things, stealing, lying, sexual immorality, and taking intoxicants, are more difficult. Every Buddhist is required to keep them as well as he can. As for the merit of wisdom and insight, rules for meditation (of which there are 42 different methods) must be followed.

Because *dana* is the most attainable merit, you will see evidence of it everywhere. Alms will be given to monks regularly and donation boxes at the pagodas are nearly always full. On the other hand, there are few facilities for looking after destitute people as charity is believed to bring greatest merit when it is directed towards the wise and morally correct, namely monks. As for beggars, tramps, orphans and delinquents, the general attitude is that it's all karma!

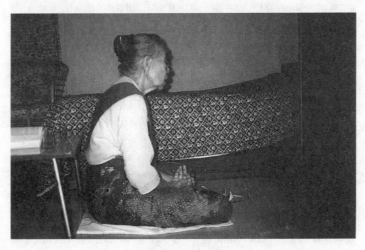

Grandma meditating.

TWO STREAMS

The political and economic situation in Burma effects nearly every one on a daily basis and has contributed to creating two very distinct outlooks on life in the minds of the Burmese. One of these is very inward-looking, turning to religion and meditation for solace. The other shows little interest in religion but focuses on economic concerns in a desperate struggle to make a living.

Certainly there appears to be much more interest in Buddhism now than, say, in the 1960s or earlier. More are interested in meditation centres, which seem to be constantly growing in number and size. Books on Buddhism have also grown in popularity as they are now available in simple Burmese, where once only those who knew the Pali language could read the scriptures.

SUPERSTITIONS

Burmese can be very superstitious, especially the womenfolk. Events will frequently be interpreted as omens and signs, and rumours are usually swallowed whole and passed on from person to person. This is to some extent due to the dire lack of media for entertainment in Burma, which only has state-owned radio, TV and newspapers.

The supernatural has always held a great fascination for the Burmese. A recent appearance of Buddha images with swollen chests caused endless rumours that the images were symbolically reflecting the sad plight of the people. Skeptics who saw the images said that the images had merely been carved that way and the rumours died down after a time. Similarly, the supernatural has been held responsible for many other events and occurrences: logs that float upstream, appearances of pagoda images in the sky, and monks levitating and travelling through the air. Of course, those who have seen these are ready to swear to their validity.

Burma is also said to possess "man-eating" rivers and lakes, so-called because of the number of drownings that have occurred in similar spots. Indeed, rivers, lakes, mountains and forests are believed by many to have spirits who should not be offended. Even J.H. Williams, the author of *Elephant Bill*, describes how he would go along with native customs when entering forests. (Williams is famous for his books on the timber-pulling elephants used in Burma.)

Certain mountains are believed to have particularly powerful spirits. Two such mountains are Mt. Popa and Mt. Kyaik-hti-yo. Believers going to such places will not take along any food that contains meat (especially pork); must not wear certain colours, such as red or black; or say certain things which are considered offensive. Any accidents that occur are believed to be due to offending the spirits by breaking one or the other of the above taboos.

Astrology, palmistry and clairvoyance are extremely popular in Burma and are relied on by most people to help make decisions about all aspects of life. Some of the more educated Burmese do, however, consider themselves above such practices and prefer science to pseudo sciences. But, in such cases, the women folk around them will probably still consult astrologers on their behalf and do whatever is necessary to avert disasters and bad luck.

The actions that need to be taken after a supernatural prediction are called *yadaya* and are expected to help offset or cancel bad luck. Such actions may include building a footbridge, mending a road, setting some fish free (usually the same number as your age) and doing other kinds of merits. Of course only the astrologer can tell you which type of action counters which kind of bad luck. Any *yadaya* which is extremely difficult or even impossible to perform usually means that you will be unable to avert an oncoming disaster.

Those who consult astrologers are therefore careful to attempt to do whatever is prescribed since they feel that if they do not take the trouble they just may get the bad luck that has been predicted. For the same reason, there are many people who do not dare go to the astrologer because they are too afraid that the *yadaya* will be beyond their power. *Yadaya* are also performed to get the girl or boy of your dreams, for a happy marriage, to get a promotion at work and so on.

Many people who are believed to have clairvoyant powers will find a long line of people on their doorstep at the break of dawn, waiting to have their fortunes told. One well-known woman in Rangoon will look at photographs to make the predictions. Another in Pegu looks at a cotton shawl while making the predictions and appears to be relating what she can see on this shawl. Another, a nun, seems to hear the predictions in her ears.

Whatever the method, each clairvoyant has a stream of clients who keep her in business. Perhaps life in Burma is more unpredictable than elsewhere or people are more insecure, but the country certainly has enough astrologers to fill the demand and there is no end to the list of psychics whom one *ought* to consult!

Experiencing Astrological Predictions

As a visitor there will always be certain experiences which are off-limits to you simply because you are a foreigner. You will be labelled a skeptic from the very beginning (especially if you're Caucasian) and many things will not be told to you because of fear of ridicule. For that matter, many Westernised Burmese also tend to reject the various superstitions that traditional Burmese hold.

If you are eager to experience an astrological or psychic prediction, you can always find out from Burmese friends if there is a fortune-teller that they could recommend or take you to. They may be happy to translate for you, although you will then find that a lot of things about your personal life will no longer be secret! It doesn't matter what's true or not true about the predictions but it does matter that many of these astrologers and palmists do not have private rooms for consultations. Everyone just sits around waiting for their turn and listens to everything! They may laugh if they hear something funny or exclaim rather ominously at other more frightening predictions. It's all a participatory process and you should be prepared to take it all in a sporting spirit.

Do not take everything too seriously; many of these fortune-tellers are experienced in human psychology more than astrology. They have an equal chance of being right or wrong about your life and, if you're a visitor, the likelihood is that you'll not be back in Burma again for a long time to tell him where he went wrong!

"BURMESENESS" OR BAMAHSAN CHINN

"Burmeseness" holds great value in Burmese eyes and being Westernised in one's speech and habits is cause for derision. *Bamahsan chinn* is a complex term and can represent a variety of things. It includes behaving with respect towards elders, being able to recite scriptures (at least the more important ones), being able to converse in idiomatic Burmese (which is very difficult and differs greatly from the written word), being indirect and subtle rather than loud and direct, dressing with modesty, being discreet in relations with the opposite sex and generally showing a knowledge of things Burmese.

Incidentally, a good living example of all of the above may be found in Aung San Suu Kyi, the leader of the National League For Democracy and current prisoner of conscience. Despite being married to an Englishman and living abroad for many years, the Nobel Prize winner holds immense popularity amongst the Burmese for her patriotism and her adherence to Burmese values. Anyone else would surely have been written-off as Westernised beyond redemption, but to hold onto Burmeseness in a foreign milieu where it is easy to forget, is highly respected.

Indeed, many expatriate Burmese are very concerned about preserving their cultural identity. This concern tends to focus on maintaining religious customs, native language and traditional behaviour as far as possible. These factors are far more important than attempting to preserve ethnic identity through marriage.

However, since being Burmese is so highly valued, mixed races, such as Eurasians who only speak English, Indians and, to a lesser extent, Chinese are generally looked down on because their customs, language and dress do not allow them to integrate fully into society.

RELATIONSHIPS

In all relationships between superiors and juniors there are set expectations on both sides. For example, parents expect obedience and filial duty, while children expect help and support from parents even into adulthood. Among relatives, the poorer usually expect some form of support or show of concern from the more wealthy.

In fact, most breakdowns in family relationships are caused by some upset in these expectations. Common examples are quarrels over inheritances, legacies, "undesirable" marriages, disrespectful children and general disobedience or uncontrollable behaviour, such as kleptomania.

Disinheritance is the usual way parents show their displeasure to their off-spring. This is intended to show that they are not responsible for the wayward behaviour of their children. By implication, then, Burmese parents do not dissociate themselves from their children when they reach adulthood and the dreaded "loss of face" can be incurred on their account (see page 65 for more on "face"). Parents continue to treat their offspring literally as children, making, or trying to make their decisions for them even as adults. On the other hand, many children are angered over the second marriage of a parent as they feel their expectations and "rights" as a child may be compromised.

Between siblings, the elder demand respect from the younger, while younger brothers and sisters expect all kinds of help from elder siblings.

In employer-employee relationships, juniors will look to their bosses as a father-figure, expecting loans in times of crisis and desperation, and for them to be understanding in times of trouble. Employees will be expected to be loyal and hard-working, and employers will generally overlook other faults if these can be obtained.

Between teacher and students, teachers are expected to supply advice, to discipline, to listen to complaints with a sympathetic ear, to advise on alternative employment and even to patch up rocky relationships. Teachers may expect their students to fulfil small errands, and to help with connections and introductions should the student go on to attain important positions in various organizations. Teachers are also expected to behave in a respectful way, for example not to have affairs with younger teachers or students.

Personal behaviour tends to colour social perceptions in Burma.

Attitudes to Male/Female Roles

In Burmese society, males have priority in everything, much the same as in other Asian cultures. This appears to derive from the belief that to be a Buddha one must first be reborn as a man. Thus, if one is born a man there is the possibility of becoming a Buddha, a Supreme Being. It doesn't matter whether he is really interested in becoming one or not. The point is that women cannot.

However, there is no heavy burden on parents when daughters are born as there is no need to pay a dowry to the bridegroom upon marriage. Girls as well as boys are regarded as "jewels", a treasured object. Nevertheless, girls are expected to look after parents more than boys. If they remain spinsters (this archaic term is still used in Burma) they will live with parents and care for them, at the same time usually supporting themselves by working as doctors, teachers, officers or clerical staff.

When boys are born, the parents rejoice that they will someday gain great merit from entering the boys into novicehood. To be parents of novices and monks is held in great esteem and is capable of bringing good karma.

Boys are lucky in that mothers, sisters and aunts will pamper them, cooking whatever they wish to eat, giving them pocket money when they are not yet earning much, washing their clothes for them and tidying up after them. Burmese women perform endless chores for men, not because they are expected to, but because they generally enjoy lavishing love and care.

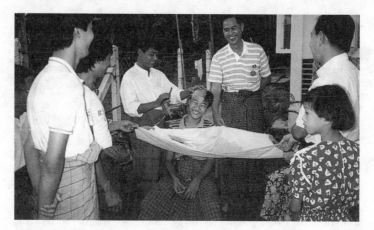

Novitiation head-shaving, proudly watched by the whole family.

Women are traditionally expected to be demure, self-effacing and unobtrusive. Girls are usually brought up to be gentle, quiet and to move with silent steps. They are not supposed to have opinions or to voice them. One can hardly find a woman in a gathering of men; women tend to group together, their interests being very different from the men.

In public, men and women tend to gather with members of the same sex. Women will go out shopping with other women friends after work, have lunch or see movies together. Men will gather at tea shops or pubs called "liquor shops" to talk about the latest news and rumours. When they do go out together in public, shows of affection between the sexes are frowned upon and are therefore rarely seen.

Friendships

Friendship is valued highly in Burma. When old friends who grew up together meet again after a period of separation, the expectation is that the friendship exists exactly as it did before. This applies regardless of the length of separation or changes in circumstances, such as success, wealth, failure or poverty. Friends from the same neighbour-hood are as close as relatives and good friends are considered part of the family.

Nevertheless, as in many other cultures, competition, bossiness and intrusive behaviour are not expected between friends in Burma. Jealousy and anger can ensue, especially over feelings that one friend is closer or more favoured than another.

Friendship also implies being privy to secrets. Some friendships are broken when confidences are not shared and hurt feelings result. Confidantes of influential and important people are especially privi-leged as some of the importance is perceived as rubbing off on them.

The lines where these expectations meet is rather fuzzy, but over-stepping or, indeed, under-stepping the mark will frequently cause upsets in relationships. Where expectations cannot be met, there are sure to be disappointments and feelings of, "after all the things I've done for you..."

EMOTIONAL PERCEPTIONS

Amongst the Burmese, perceptions tend to be emotional rather than rational, and subjective rather than objective.

For example, criticism is nearly always taken as a personal insult. It is also hard for objective analysis to come into personal situations. A marriage-guidance counsellor would never be consulted in a shaky marriage as such a person is considered a total stranger and could not possibly understand the situation as family and friends could. The very idea of consulting a stranger about personal problems is unac-ceptable, so counsellors of the psychological kind do not exist in Burma.

Elders or those in authority within the family or community are always considered right and are above criticism from juniors.

Face

Loss of face socially is intolerable and the one who causes it will usually meet with some kind of "penalty". However, losing face is seldom held to be so great that one would commit suicide, as in certain cultures. Burmese are generally an easy-going race and seldom hold loss of face as a long-term grievance or vendetta. They can be quite philosophical about circumstances and do not let themselves be upset for long.

Loss of face can be caused by anyone, but particularly by the behaviour of children, subordinates or any kind of junior. Criticism, disagreement and contradiction from a junior is likely to cause a loss of face. Juniors feel *ah-nar-de* (see below) if they criticise seniors. They must save seniors a loss of face at all costs, even when gross or glaring errors are being made by the latter.

Ah-nar-hmu *and* Ah-nar-de

Ah-nar-de or *ah-nar-hmu* is a feeling which has often been described as a national trait. It is a feeling of not wanting to impose on others, wanting to give in when one can, not wanting to cause trouble or loss of face. For example, when seconds are served at a meal, it is polite to refuse once or twice before being pressed to have some more. To those who are direct, this custom is very tiresome.

The feeling of *ah-nar-de* is also responsible for the refusal to contradict or disagree with those regarded as superior in rank or age. If something must be said, it has to be done in private.

However, older people also feel *ah-nar-de*. For example, parents living with their children will feel it when they fall sick. They will often suffer in silence to avoid causing the trouble of having to be taken to the doctor or hospital.

Between friends *ah-nar-hmu* (noun) means giving in to each other whenever reasonable requests are made. However, when demands become excessive, the feeling is that the other party is lacking *ah-nar-hmu*.

Ah-nar-hmu causes great difficulties in human relationships and one has to watch how far one goes. Prevarication, white lies and evasiveness are all part of the behaviour. It may seem hypocritical but, among Burmese, those who are blunt and direct usually make others cringe.

Such direct people are the exception and are not considered very Burmese in their behaviour.

Empathy (Ko Chinn Sar-Nar-Hmu)

A feeling that also plays a part in Burmese relationships is that of empathy, referred to as *ko chinn sar-nar-hmu*. The ability to not only sympathise, but actually feel the same way as a friend or member of the family is feeling, helps greatly in consoling others during hard times such as bereavements. Friends are actually expected to be empathetic in crises and saying things that are stoical or lacking in empathy causes ill-will.

Superiors are also expected to show empathy towards their juniors in times of trouble. For example, employers should not assign duties that require husbands and wives to live apart, they should not refuse to give leave when it is needed on emotional grounds and they should try to have realistic expectations of their subordinates in terms of work and achievements.

Generally, the feeling is one of consideration to others.

ENVIRONMENTAL PERCEPTIONS

Because Burma has always been a land of abundance, with creeks and rivers full of fish, plenty of trees with edible leaves and fruit, and rice easily grown, Burmese do not have much concern for tomorrow. Neither do they give much thought to the day when all of these will be depleted. Trees are cut down at random and wood and water are wasted. Food is also thrown away as the Burmese like to cook fresh food at each mealtime. To some extent the lack of refrigeration accounts for this habit.

The general perception of the people is that everything that grows in the environment belongs to anyone who can make use of it. Thus,

67

Flower sellers at market.

one can see whole branches of flowering trees cut down for their blooms which are sold as hair decorations or for offerings to the Buddha. Poverty has made this tendency worse so that you may find people cutting the flowers in your garden or trying to get at the fruit on your trees. Perhaps this attitude derives from the behaviour of the kings who were absolute monarchs over the country and all its products. V.C. Scott O'Connor (*Mandalay and Other Cities of the Past in Burma*) describes how, "The land and what it offered was thus perceived as a giant estate, there for the taking."

Appreciation of beauty has never been high on the list of Burmese refinements. To leave a tree full of blossoms and not to sell a single flower is considered foolish and to view flowers just for their beauty is equally ridiculous.

Chapter Four

GETTING TO KNOW
THE BURMESE

At the present time it is quite difficult for any foreigner to get to know Burmese freely. A visitor's capacity to familiarise themselves with Burmese friends in their own homes among family and relatives is circumscribed in very strict ways by the government. Officials are placed under even greater restrictions, their relationships with foreigners being limited to official duties and no more. Indeed, all meetings with foreigners require reports to be submitted. Staying as a guest in someone's home for any period of time has to be reported to local authorities, even if the visitor is another Burmese. So it is not common for the Burmese to invite foreigners to their homes for overnight stays or even dinner.

Of course there are always ways and means of getting to know Burmese people, even if it's only through chatting to a trishaw driver, street vendor or anyone else you may encounter on your travels.

The younger generation, perhaps as a reaction to having grown up in a closed environment, are generally eager to make acquaintances with foreigners. They usually show a genuine desire to help foreigners appreciate the beautiful aspects of their country, although the little gifts they may receive in the process are, of course, an added bonus. Any chance of being able to practice their English is also appreciated, as most youngsters learn the language in conversation classes, known as "English-speaking classes".

If, however, the person you speak to appears nervous and disinterested, it is best not to press further but simply try someone else.

Do be careful to avoid discussions about political issues, which can prove to be dangerous for yourself and for the locals. Even if the people you speak to complain about politics or the economy, it is safer to be discreet than valorous. Also avoid religious discussions and criticism as the Burmese can get very worked up over what they believe to be religious insults.

THE BURMESE PERSONALITY

Burmese have been variously described as open, gay, informal, childlike, and carefree. On the other hand, they have also been described as arrogant, boastful, proud, secretive and paranoid, with extreme distrust of those perceived as rivals or competitors.

Both groups of descriptions are true and seem to depend mainly on situations. If outsiders are involved it seems that the latter traits take over. In other words, all situations involving foreigners are perceived as potentially threatening. Perhaps this is one reason why the country has remained closed for so long.

Rulers of the past have been particularly prone to this type of paranoid behaviour, frequently resorting to murder to rid themselves of rivals and competitors (usually half-brothers and sisters, as kings had many queens). Murdering uncles, aunts and even fathers was also not uncommon amongst royalty. Indeed, a Burmese proverb states that, "When clearing the reeds, one should never overlook the stumps and roots."

Slights, real or perceived, may be reciprocated with added viciousness or lead to grudges. This may be the result of not treating superiors with due respect; indirect comments which are interpreted as insults; or various gestures and body language which are interpreted as snubs.

The man on the street is generally good-humoured, patient and appears to be easy-going in his attitude. But he is often hurt by criticism, by rejection (especially when he has gone out of his way to do something) and usually will be infuriated by what he regards as presumptuousness or one-up-manship. The latter may include being overtaken on the road, being patronised or looked down on, or deliberately snubbed. Most murders in Burma are said not to be premeditated but rather the result of spur-of-the-moment bursts of anger, when any weapon to hand is seized during an exchange of hot words.

However, most Burmese are content if they have three meals a day, with rice as the staple. Not everyone wishes to be a millionaire but they do need to have enough to eat and to be able to make a decent living. Being very wealthy is not the aim; leading a morally correct life according to the Five Precepts is more important.

Nevertheless, as inflation becomes hyperinflation, corruption is inevitable. Much of this may be due to the fact that the scale of pay used during the years after independence (1948) was only adjusted in the late 1980s. The adjustment simply involved the printing of more money and this was not proportionate to the increase in goods and services. Petty theft and pilfering, especially of objects such as paper, pens, clips, neon lights and switches, is not uncommon, particularly in government offices. Even manhole covers have been known to mysteriously disappear. Though the Burmese acknowledge this as morally wrong, it can be rationalised as being done out of necessity and the need to survive.

Clans and gangs, popular in other Asian cultures, are not common in Burma as it is generally each for himself. Burmese are usually very individualistic and it is commonly remarked that two Burmese can be friends but three will be enemies.

This individualism is culturally acceptable as there is no great emphasis on carrying on the family line, producing male heirs or worshipping ancestors. Graves are not particularly maintained and, in fact, it appears that the Burmese are reluctant to visit cemeteries unless absolutely necessary. Any remembrance of deceased family members is mostly through performing good deeds in their honour and holding "merit transference" ceremonies which involve feeding monks, giving alms and conducting other charitable acts.

Rural lifestyles, defined by the seasons, have remained the same for centuries.

URBAN VS RURAL

You may not have a chance to meet Burmese villagers as travel is permitted to certain areas only, at least at the present time. If you do manage to get around, the kind of people you are likely to meet in urban areas differ considerably from those in the villages.

The urban educated are mostly those who have graduated from one of the universities. They are likely to be professionals such as accountants, engineers, doctors, teachers and lawyers. Some will also be clerical staff, but even these may have a degree as education is highly valued and everyone will aim for further education if they have the chance. However, employment is difficult and most graduates have to work in whatever jobs are available. Many degree holders and professionals are even in daily wage jobs, supplementing their income by moonlighting.

In government jobs, it used to be common to find staff away from their desks most of the time, especially under the socialist government when many people were involved in party activities and could produce this excuse at any time. What was usually the case was that the person concerned would be preoccupied with personal business, such as queuing up at some store to buy something that had a resale value and then reselling that item on the black market for a much higher price. Queuing was the order of the day because of goods being sold on a rationed basis and, consequently, a great deal of time was spent away from work. All the energy needed for this activity seems to have been far more worthwhile than working at a regular job with a very low pay.

In the urban areas there is congestion and over-crowding. Life is hectic, especially as most city-dwellers seem to feel the pressures of struggling to make a living more keenly than villagers. Of course, young people from the rural areas are drawn to the towns and the capital.

In Burma a number of villages are grouped into village tracts. Being a rural country, only eight out of 400 towns have a population of more than 100 000 and only Rangoon, Mandalay and Moulmein would qualify as cities.

Rural people live a simple life, as they have done for many generations. Agriculture is their main livelihood, although in the border areas they may also trade in the black market. Traditional villagers are an older generation, most of whom lived through the Second World War. The kind of values they hold are more distinctly Buddhist: belief in karma, in hell and strict adherence to the Five Precepts.

The seasons probably define villagers' lives more than anything else as livelihoods depend on agriculture. Sometimes a living can be made from other traditional crafts like pottery and weaving.

Leisure and entertainment for the villagers mainly consists of ceremonies for novitiation and monkhood, the pagoda festivals, touring theatre groups and open-air movies. Most of these activities take place during the cool, dry seasons, before or after the rainy agricultural season.

Generally, the life of villagers has been the same for centuries. Radios, TVs, movies, cars and bicycles are probably the only symbols of modernity. Villagers, however, remain alienated from politics, not knowing who their leaders are or how they are governed. What is more important to them is that a good price is offered for their crops so they can make a reasonable living.

Urban Homes

An average urban Burmese home will be raised on four posts and have a concrete base. It has two or three rooms which are usually partitioned only with plywood or asbestos sheets that have cotton curtains in place of doors.

The main room, as you climb up a short flight of steps, is the living room which often contains an altar. This may be in a recess in one wall or on a small shelf at head level. Here the family's Buddha image is kept surrounded by flowers in vases, votive water cups and candles.

In the morning the family will also offer fruit, small cups of cooked rice or other food. Because the altar is in this room it is usual for guests to remove shoes when entering.

A set of light wooden chairs with woven cane seats are for guests. There is usually a small coffee table and peg tables. Plastic rather than fresh flowers are used for decoration, more from economy than preference. Instead of paintings and pictures, the Burmese like to decorate their walls with calendars and photos of deceased grandparents, parents and graduate children in their caps and gowns. They particularly love calendars, especially of colourful foreign scenes, pets or flowers. Calendars make a good gift as they are only sold at New Year on the black market (i.e. the sidewalks of streets).

Most homes have a showcase   a sideboard with glass doors   in which various dolls, souvenirs and presents are displayed. Sometimes dinnersets and coffeesets, new pots, kettles and even electrical appliances may be put on show.

You may also notice that the refrigerator is kept in the dining room. This is because the kitchen is usually too far away or is too small for it. Sometimes it is also because servants are just too rough to be allowed to handle such an expensive appliance.

It is common to find that guests are entertained with photo albums. The Burmese are very fond of having photos taken at pagodas, parks and beaches, and they love to show them to friends. Women and girls like to strike poses when having their photos taken. Indeed, photographers can make a modest living from hanging around pagodas and public places.

Villages

Every village has a monastery, cemetery and sometimes a school. However, clinics or hospitals would be in the nearest town.

Each village traditionally has a headman who has to solve social problems such as quarrels and fights, and liaise with government authorities.

75

In some parts of Burma, villagers have to go quite a distance to collect water.

A typical village hut is made of thatch and may have walls of bamboo matting. A wooden house, often with a corrugated iron roof, is for the more affluent. Some old houses in the villages are splendid sights, with whole tree trunks for the main pillars. Traditionally, mahogany or teak wood was used for housing but such wood is now difficult to find. All of the houses and huts are raised several feet above the ground because of floods during rainy seasons.

In recent times, many villages show a noticeable lack of young people. This is because, if parents can afford it, youngsters are sent to the towns and cities to study at colleges and universities or to learn a "modern" trade. Alternatively, the young are lured to the cities in search of work and better prospects.

Family life

Family ties are strong in Burma and families tend to be extended rather than nuclear. It is not uncommon to find grandparents, uncles, aunts and cousins all living under the same roof. Privacy is therefore minimal. Each member of the family is expected to contribute in some way towards either the expenses or the running of the household.

In the family the father is usually a distant but loving figure; the traditional and ideal attitude of children towards parents has been formulated as "love, fear, respect". It is the mother who is usually closest to the children, together with aunts (usually her sisters). Most approaches to the father will be channelled through the mother, although for important or difficult issues the mother will often defer decisions with the common saying, "Ask your father." While the father rarely gets involved in bringing up children or domestic problems, he will take the lead in leisure activities for the family, which usually consist of outings to pagodas, monasteries, parks and the cinema.

The day-to-day running of the household, including expenses, is done by the mother and any other relatives staying in the same home. The whole month's salary will be handed over by the father to the mother who will divide the sum according to various expenses. These often include giving parents-in-law a monthly allowance, making charity donations to important causes and handling children's expenses.

Relatives who come to visit, for however long, are welcomed. Indeed, they are expected to stay with the family as, among the Burmese, hotels are for foreigners. However, in return for this hospitality they are expected to help wherever they can. They may show their appreciation by looking after the children, teaching them, helping with meals or going along with the mother when she shops. Any domestic staff will also do the same, either for a salary or in return for lessons, clothes and meals, all of which they may have struggled to get back home in their own villages.

In urban areas there are now many smaller nuclear families consisting of the parents, child and maid. Managing such a family may seem easier, with fewer mouths to feed and certainly more privacy. But, in fact, such an arrangement often leads to a lower quality of life for all concerned as working parents struggle to get by without the help, advice and pooled contributions of an extended family.

Women in Burma

The role of women in Burmese society has often been discussed in books on Burma. Burmese women have been described as "self-possessed, confident and capable". *The World of Burmese Women* by Daw Mi Mi Khaing is a comprehensive account of various aspects of the life of Burmese women.

Their role is perceived by Westerners to be equal to the male role, although supportive and complementary to it rather than in competition. There are no movements for women's rights since education is readily available, women can enter any profession they wish and can own property. They do not need to change their names after marriage and, in the event of divorce, half of the property accumulated after the marriage can be claimed. If they accept a role a step behind their menfolk they do so freely and willingly.

It is only in religious matters women have to take second place to men. However, even here they are still able to do important work as providers, carers and meal planners at monasteries and meditation centres.

Education is very highly valued by parents, so daughters are educated right up to graduate level if it can be afforded. Statistics show that more than half the population at Burmese universities are girls.

Girls also tend to obtain high marks at college by dint of sheer hard work. They are also able to enter the more prestigious courses and colleges, such as medical college, under a system which selects university entrants by marks alone. Unfortunately, although doctors are still in demand and have considerable earning power, the lack of good practices and the scarcity of drugs and medical equipment has meant frustrating situations for medics. Regardless of this, sexual

Even young girls help to supplement the family income. This one, wearing traditional thanaka powder, has a cloth on her head to balance her tray of wares.

equality within medicine and other prestigious professions is not an issue as women receive the same salaries and privileges as men.

In the medical profession women tend to become obstetricians, gynaecologists, paediatricians (particularly appropriate because of the taboo on touching between the sexes) or eye surgeons and dentists. Women surgeons, architects and engineers are rather few but these professions are still open to those who wish to enter. The legal profession is not a viable career at present since it has been superseded by a system of directives and orders from the government.

Maternity leave is usually one and a half months before birth and one to two months after delivery. Most mothers try to work as long as they can before the birth so that they can take most of their entitled leave afterwards.

Burmese women are characteristically shrewd and practical but do not make pretensions towards intellectual matters. It is generally left to

79

the men to gather and discuss politics and social matters. Women tend towards the telling of anecdotes and practical matters, such as the exchange of recipes and discussions about problems with children.

Traditionally the most valued combination in marriage was that of the husband in a government job that gave status and prestige, and the wife supplementing the husband's income by running a home business, such as making preserved fruits or cheroot (local cigarettes). It is also not uncommon for women to act as money-lenders or brokers for the sale of jewellery. Indeed, for most Burmese women, business seems to come naturally.

This is still true, but at the present time these job choices are increasingly changing due to the fact that government careers are no longer as highly paid as they used to be. Therefore, both men and women are now entering business ventures or looking for a way to do so by searching for contacts. Most are interested in trade rather than production or agriculture. Trade is perceived as a lucrative source of income because of the precedence of the black market which earned considerable fortunes for those who were willing to take risks. Manufacturing is seen to be time-consuming and requiring more skill and expertise. It takes time to establish contacts in this field and the whole process from raw materials to finished product requires great patience. It seems that most people are very impatient because of the long years of hardship under the socialist system. Manufacturing and agriculture both need years of input and labour before substantial returns can be seen.

For single and unskilled young women from the villages, domestic work is the most common vocation beyond agricultural labour. Nevertheless, if manufacturing was developed in Burma, a trend for these young girls to be drawn to factory work is likely to develop. This is because domestic jobs offer no real rights to the employee who, in return for long hours, is rarely given fixed leave, medical insurance or even much freedom of movement for fear that they will make contacts with the outside world.

ATTITUDES TO THE WEST

In the past, Burmese kings considered Burma the centre of the earth. Their court has been described as the most arrogant in the world. In fact, in 1287 King Narathihapate executed a whole delegation representing the Chinese ruler Kublai Khan. However, he eventually had to flee Kublai Khan's armies, thus earning himself the name *Tayoke-pyay-min* or "the king who fled from the Chinese".

Foreigners are generally well-treated as long as they are only visiting and not perceived as a threat. If prejudice exists, it is chiefly towards South Asians. This problem appears to have stemmed from the large scale migration of Indian labour during the colonial period. Later, frequent clashes between Indians and Burmese took place. Even now, the Chettiars (a class of Indian moneylenders) are seen as the epitome of stinginess in Burma as they are blamed for making many landlords forfeit their land when loans could not be repaid.

Despite being a British colony for about 100 years, the majority of Burmese did not have any strong desire to ape the British or to be Anglophiles. The only exception to this was a small group of Western-educated elite. These often included doctors and engineers who would dress in Western clothes for work. However, this applied only to the men; Burmese women have never worn dresses (called *ga-won* from "gown"), despite living under the British. Even today, the Western-educated may speak English quite often and show a taste for things Western in their home decor or in their preferences for food and drink, but essentially they never give up their Burmese identity. Religion-wise, Buddhism was never abandoned nor Christianity embraced with the arrival of Western education and Westernisation.

Nevertheless, the arts, literature and theatre have all flourished since Western influences crept in. This has generally taken the form of adaptations and modifications to the Burmese language under the influence of English, and novels and poetry began to be written in new and more direct language. However, extensive writings in English itself have not appeared much.

Many Burmese are wary of foreigners, but still show an interest in foreign news. Here, they are looking at US election results.

In the rural areas Western influence is even less. English would probably be understood, but only those words that have crept into the Burmese language might be spoken. "Yes", "no", "thank you" and "sorry" are quite commonly used.

One still might encounter awe amongst the rural Burmese over Western inventions such as the telephone, television, cameras and cassette recorders, but there is certainly no great desire to behave like Westerners. In other words, Western behaviour is not perceived as worthy of imitation.

Many of the more Westernised Burmese tend to lead double lives, behaving appropriately according to the situation and setting. Some even have two accents to deal with two vastly different sets of people.

Those of mixed cultural origins, such as Eurasians with a mix of British-Indian or British-Burmese blood, were usually looked down on. Most of these people left Burma in the 1960s and early 1970s. They were not inclined to speak Burmese, preferred to speak English and wear Western clothes, and therefore could not be assimilated. The general feeling toward them was that they wished to appear Western because the West was more developed - an accusation that they were attempting to rise above their station.

Others of mixed blood, like the Sino-Burmese or Indo-Burmese, are on the whole rather well assimilated with Burmese communities. They wear Burmese dress, speak Burmese and have adopted Burmese names.

The Meaning of "Closed"

Burma has been closed to foreign visitors for nearly three decades. It is usually very hard for Westerners, who are used to ideas of democracy and human rights, to imagine what "closed" really implies. In the case of Burma, "closed" means that visas are granted to foreign visitors only for brief periods of a week or two and then only specific areas of the country can be visited. In this way, the numbers of tourists and other visitors to Burma have been limited.

Those Burmese who emigrated and took citizenship in other countries were not allowed to visit the country even on humanitarian grounds, such as the death of a parent.

In terms of business, there has been virtually no interest in obtaining foreign investment. The government was more preoccupied with self-sufficiency, so foreign entrepreneurs have been few and far between. It has only been very recently (since the late 1980s) that foreign investors have been actively sought.

Another way in which Burma is closed is in the availability of media of any kind. Imports of books and magazines have been so limited that they reach only a selected few and, then again, only those with an English education (namely graduates up to the mid 1960s) can read English with proficiency. Bookshops selling English books are few. The ones that do exist in the big cities sell or loan novels and magazines rather than textbooks, technical books or non-fiction titles

83

of general interest. Consequently, there is a great thirst for books. However, gifts of books from abroad are never likely to reach their destination but end up on the streets to be peddled at black market prices.

There is one English newspaper which carries only "safe" news items. The same situation exists with national TV. There is only one channel and it starts in the evening or slightly earlier on weekends and public holidays. Satellite news is shown, but only the more "neutral" news items. The real link that the people have with the rest of the world is the radio (the BBC and VOA).

It appears that the radio is listened to avidly by everyone. In fact, news in Burma is so dull that newspapers are read mainly for the obituaries. Other articles mostly cover meetings of government leaders and a few items of foreign news translated into Burmese. Most news items are so heavy on political rhetoric that they fail to be meaningful, although this is not as bad as in the days of the socialist period when a good deal of Marxist terms like "exploitation of the people", "working class" and "profiteering" were used.

Mail from abroad is usually censored and many letters are received stuck back with glue.

People, of course, never write or say anything of importance in mail or telephone communication. They all appear to have other means which circumvent the system.

The Black Market

The black market is perhaps one of the few industries that has actually flourished during the closed years. This is because the borders with India, China and Thailand are extensive and porous, with many passes through the mountain ranges. In fact, due to the poor quality and lack of government produced goods, many consumers are thankful for the existence of the black market, without which they would hardly have had anything to wear, use, eat or drink.

Consumer articles of all types are therefore in great demand, from

T-shirts, Levi jeans and Reebok shoes to cosmetics and lace materials. These articles can all be found on the black market, as long as you can afford the extortionate prices. Of course, the black marketeers make fortunes from their activities and, despite the doubtful origins of their wealth, they have fast become a class of powerful *nouveau riche*.

Foreign Exchange

The F.E. or "Effee" is a magic word in Burma. As it is frequently bandied about, you may wonder what it actually means. It is, in fact, an abbreviation for "foreign exchange" which is always at a premium, even though it is officially illegal to own any within the country. As stated in Chapter One, visitors are given foreign exchange certificates at banks, but the reality is (at least at the present time) that on the black market the US dollar fetches about K140, more than twenty times the official rate!

Anybody who has a chance to go abroad is therefore regarded as extremely lucky and it is assumed that he is sure to make a fortune! The latter preconceived notion makes nearly every youth long to become seamen as salaries would be paid in valuable F.E. A scholarship awarded to a civil servant by some foreign agency is to be greatly coveted and competitively vied for.

These extremes in attitude are the natural results of living in a place so isolated from neighbouring countries that the latter have come to be conceived as a kind of financial paradise. Of course, some Burmese do have contacts with foreign countries, either through business or relatives who have migrated. Many aspire to live, be educated or work abroad. But generally such people have a high standard of education and are living in the larger cities. The majority, especially those living in rural areas, do not care about or know anything of foreign places, people and things. It would not make a great difference to them whether they consumed foreign products or not, as essentials are more in need.

Attitudes to Foreigners

The many restrictions on contacts with the outside world means that foreigners are always regarded as foreigners *per se*. Caucasians in particular stick out like sore thumbs and may be followed around by idle young people who will find everything they do most interesting, just like a show being put on for their benefit. Especially in public places, there are always groups of such people around. It is certainly very hard to become part of the crowd in Burma, given the rarity of tourists.

Staring is also something you will have to put up with. The Burmese will stare at each other and at anything unusual, even the handicapped or deformed.

There appears to be a great fascination and awe for things foreign, but this is coupled with a distrust or watchful tolerance. One should remember that a whole generation of Burmese has reached its mid-twenties without having set eyes on many foreigners or had any interaction with them. For them the only knowledge of things foreign comes from television, translated books or magazine articles written by those who have access to foreign literature of some kind. (Some of these articles and books are quite poorly translated. One comes across guinea pigs translated as "pigs from Guinea" and grapefruit juice as synonymous with "grapejuice"!)

Expectations of Foreigners

On the other hand, foreigners are also seen as links with the outside world. They are therefore perceived as sources for finding jobs abroad, as couriers to and from the country and also as providers of highly valued consumer items (especially ballpoint pens, T shirts, chocolates and books).

Of course, hardly any foreigner who visits can fulfil all of these expectations, but one should be aware that they seem to exist behind most contacts that are made.

In business, foreigners are perceived as having unlimited funds, as having endless knowledge to teach locals all the newest techniques, systems and methods, and, of course, as being morally loose.

There is no doubt that as the number of Burmese going abroad grows and the number of visitors to Burma does likewise, the extremes in attitudes towards foreigners and things foreign will change. People will begin to see that foreign places have their good points as well as their bad, and that Burma itself is just the same.

NAMES

Burmese names can be very confusing to visitors as certain prefixes and honorifics are required. The Burmese generally have no surname or family name and you will come across various combinations of names which will totally confuse you. For example there may be two people, one called U Khin Thein and another called U Thein Khin; or a husband and wife, one called U Aye Hla and the other Daw Hla Aye.

How can foreigners cope with such names? First let's look at how they are chosen.

The Naming System

Traditionally the Burmese choose names for their children according to the day of the week on which a child is born. Each day of the week is assigned certain letters of the Burmese alphabet. Some common names for each day are:

Monday	Kyaw, Khin, Kyin, Kyi, Ngway.
Tuesday	San, Sann, Su, Soe, Nyi, Nyein.
Wednesday	Lin, Win, Hla, Yee.
Thursday	May, Ba, Mya, Maung, Myint, Myo.
Friday	Than, Thein, Thaung, Thinn, Han.
Saturday	Yin, Tun (pronounced "toon"), Nu, Nwe.
Sunday	Ohn, Aye, Ee, Aung.

Burmese names are formed through a combination of these names of the week. Certain days of the week are also thought to be compatible. For example a girl born on Thursday could be named Myint Myint San as Thursday and Tuesday are compatible. A boy could be called Myo Tun, Thursday and Saturday being compatible.

For the purpose of finding out on which day of the week a person was born there is a calendar book which lists 100 year periods and shows the Burmese lunar calendars as well. This volume is produced from time to time to include the latest years.

However, not all Burmese parents will follow this naming system. Some will consult an astrologer who will help in choosing the most auspicious name for their child, according to the time of its birth.

Names can also be changed in mid-life when some severe misfortune or bad luck affects a person. Changes in names are announced in the newspaper and registration cards can hold a number of aliases if a person has frequently changed his/her name! It's certainly a confusing system, especially when you meet an acquaintance or friend who no longer has the same name you previously knew them by.

The father's name or a part of it may sometimes be included in the child's name. For example, U Thein Aung's son may be named Aung Win and his daughter Hla Hla Thein. It is very unlikely that you would find a father and son with exactly the same name. You may, however, find a husband and wife with the same name or a reversal of the same name, such as U Tin Hla being married to Daw Hla Tin. This is certainly confusing, but it is usually only a coincidence as a married woman does not change her name upon marriage.

In the case of Aung San Suu Kyi, there is an exception to the rule as the whole father's name has been placed at the front. Kyi, which is part of the mother's name (Daw Khin Kyi), has also been included, while her own name, Suu, is in the centre. The reason for placing her father's name at the front is because he was a national leader and hero.

Western Names
During the colonial period and early post-independence years it was usual for Burmese children to have English as well as Burmese

names. This was especially the case for those who went to missionary schools where foreign priests and nuns would choose English names so that they could be more easily remembered and pronounced.

Shirley Temple, the actress, appears to have inspired a whole crop of Burmese Shirleys. There also are many Elisabeths and Margarets, while George, Michael, Peter and John were quite common names chosen for males in urban areas.

Some families have also developed the habit of calling their children Baby and Sonny, which can sound quite odd when they are addressed as Auntie Baby and Uncle Sonny in later life.

Trends

From the mid-1960s to the present day, the trend has been for children to have only Burmese names, as anything of a foreign nature has been strongly discouraged by the government.

Some male children are given the names of historically important people or those of courtiers and royalty, all of which differ from the names commoners had during monarchical times.

Among Christian families, Christian names are commonly used. The Karen, who were converted to Christianity by the earliest missionaries, usually choose Biblical names such as Moses, Joseph, Daniel, Mary or Ruth.

Honorifics

These must be placed in front of names to indicate status or rank. The honorifics change according to the status of an individual.

	Male	Female
child	Maung (abbr. Mg)	Ma
young adult	Ko	Ma
working adult	U (pron. "oo" not "you")	Daw
teacher or boss	Saya	Sayama

Other honorifics that you may come across are ethnic titles of status:

	Male	Female
Shan royalty	Sao (Burmese Saw)	Sao (Burmese Saw)
Shan	Sai	Nang
Karen	Saw	Nan
Mon	Mahn, Mehm or Nai	Mi
Chin	Sai	(no female equivalent)
Kachin ruler	Duwa	(no female equivalent)

Excessive pressure to "Burmanise" has resulted in the addition of U and Daw to the above prefixes. For example a Karen employee, Saw Tha Htoo, might be called U Saw Tha Htoo in the office, although the prefix U is actually redundant here.

Sometimes you will see the following prefix titles conferred upon government officials or members of state as a token of respect for long or meritorious service:

Maha Thray Sithu

Sithu

Thiri Pyan Chi

Wunna Kyaw Htin

Naing-ngant Gon-yi (placed at the end of the name, in brackets)

Difficulties of the Naming System

In filling up forms it is quite common for Burmese to be asked to give the names of grandparents, uncles, aunts, brothers and sisters. Foreigners asked to fill up similar documents when applying for a visa cannot understand the need to know the names of their entire family as usually only the Christian names would vary.

For example, one U Thein Aung might consider his surname to be Aung, while another might consider the whole name Thein Aung to be the surname, in which case they would be filed under the letters A and T respectively.

Outside Burma, a simple act like trying to call a Burmese friend at a hotel can turn into an ordeal when one doesn't know how he may have registered himself. The computer system may have even filed him under U.

Airlines have even been known to file women under Daw and men under U which is equivalent to filing them under Mrs, Miss or Mr!

Who are you?

As Burmese society has been rather immobile up to the present, it has generally been possible to place a person and establish his identity despite the lack of family names. The usual way to do this is to ask a person which town he comes from, who his parents are, what they do and so on.

Some successful people put the name of the province or town of birth in front of their names. For example, Kanbawza Khin Hlaing (a well-known doctor and writer), has the old name for the Shan states as a prefix. Similarly, Pantanaw U Khant (brother of former UN Secretary General U Thant) puts his home town in front of his name. This brings honour and recognition to one's place of birth as well as establishing identity. Many authors and poets have used this kind of prefix in combination with their names or pseudonyms. Obituaries will also state the town of origin of the deceased to be sure of identity.

As education is so highly valued it is also quite common to find the word *Tekkatho*, meaning "university", in front of many names, thus showing that the person is a graduate. One well-known actor, who has since passed away, was known as Collegian Ne Win because he went to college and also made a famous movie entitled *Collegian*. Some graduates use the prefix *Theippan*, meaning "science", showing that either they specialise in science writing or are trained as scientists.

Even though such identification clues are attached to names, it is still very common to find large organizations full of employees with the same name. In some companies, personnel even have to be given numbers to avoid confusion!

You and I, Uncle and Auntie

The Burmese have specific ways of addressing each other depending on the parties involved. Every social relationship, be it that of a teacher and student, a monk and his disciple, a friend and a friend, a parent and a child, or a superior and a subordinate, involves different forms of address.

Certain words are used in place of the pronouns "you" and "I". For instance, instead of simply saying the pronoun "you", they use terms that are the equivalent of "my master", "thou" or the person's name. "I" could be "your humble servant", "daughter/son" (if talking to an older person), or just your own name. Females, especially, would use their own name in every sentence. For example, a girl named Hla could say, "Hla is going out now." The Burmese words for "you" and "I" are actually only used in a more formal setting.

Among convent-bred, English-educated women it is quite common to intersperse sentences in Burmese with the English terms, "you" and "I". However, this type of conversation is usually considered pretentious and is the object of derision among conservative Burmese.

Kinship titles are used among close friends, even though they are not actually related to each other. Such titles are:

Elder brother	Ah ko
Elder sister	Ma ma
Eldest brother	Ahko gyi ("gyi" is pronounced "ji")
Eldest sister	Ahma gyi
Younger brother	Nyi
Younger sister	Nyi ma
Uncle	U
Aunt	Daw

The use of the English words "uncle" and "aunty" as honorifics for those of a certain age is quite common, especially when addressing friends of one's parents. However, in the rural areas it would be more proper to address elders of a village as U rather than the English "uncle".

To avoid offence do not address mature women as "aunty" which can be misconstrued as implying great age. It is better to use the formal Daw in such cases.

Ways to Address Your Counterpart

Bearing in mind this complexity of names and honorifics, visitors may worry about how to address their Burmese colleagues. Let's look at a concrete example which shows how forms of address vary.

U Hla Shein, the General Manager of a company, could be addressed as:

U Hla Shein by business colleagues;

Ko Hla Shein by colleagues of a long-standing nature;

Ko Hla by his wife;

Maung Hla Shein by his teachers, monks of his hometown monastery and elders.

As a foreigner, however, you should address him as U Hla Shein on the first meeting, that is until and unless he gives you a specific way to address him.

He may allow you to call him either Hla or Shein to make things easier for you, but he will never be addressed in this manner by his Burmese friends. If you add the honorific U (or Daw for a woman) to the name you will generally find that regard for you is very high indeed.

Do not try to show friendliness or closeness by using a name without a prefix as this can easily be misunderstood as an insult or show of disrespect. You should use the formal prefix until your counterpart asks you to drop it.

Ways You May be Addressed

Conversely, it is extremely hard for Burmese to drop honorific forms of address to those whom they perceive as being superior in education, age, rank or status. Dr John Smith, for example, will be called Dr John by his patients and students, but never just John, even if he should insist on it. The use of the Christian name alone sounds rude and disrespectful to the Burmese ear, and even more so is the use of the surname only.

So it may be that your Burmese counterpart keeps on calling you Dr, Mr, Miss or Mrs much to your annoyance and you may make the mistake of thinking that you have been unable to reach a level of informality at all. The real reason for addressing you this way is actually to show respect and deference.

GREETINGS

Among the Burmese it is not usual to greet each other with "good morning", "good day", "goodnight" or "goodbye". Greetings would be rhetorical questions like, "Where are you going?", "Have you eaten your meal?" and "Are you well?" An answer (or an exact one, at least) is not needed and a smile in return would be sufficient. Between two women the conversation may be as inane as saying to each other, "You've put on/lost weight," especially if they have not seen each other for some time.

In recent times the phrase *mingala-ba*, meaning something like "auspiciousness be upon you", has been used in schools by pupils greeting their teachers every morning. It is not used very widely elsewhere, although most Burmese would be charmed to find a foreign visitor greeting them with this phrase.

How Do You Do?

A humorous story about a famous dancer and his troupe visiting the USA in the 1950s tells about the dancer being greeted with a "How do you do?", whereupon he raised his arms in a typical dancing pose and replied, "I do like this!"

Probably a simple "hello" is sure to be understood by everyone as even Burmese use it when answering phones.

Thank You and Sorry

It is not usual in Burmese to say "thank you" for every service and "sorry" for every mistake. To show that one is sorry, it is more acceptable to say "forgive me" or admit that a mistake was inadvertent. To express thanks, actions like returning gifts or performing some sort of service are appreciated more than words. English-educated people would, however, be likely to say "thank you" and "sorry" in English and if you use these terms you will be understood by everyone.

Nevertheless, the Burmese terms to express thanks or apology are:

kyay zu tin bar de	thank you
kyay zu bar be	thank you
seik ma shi bar ne	literally, please do not get angry
khwint hlut par	literally, do forgive me

LANGUAGE

In Burma the official language is Burmese. It is used in most offices but sometimes forms and receipts are still in English. Often they are the same as those used since the 1950s. Signs on shops are usually in both Burmese and English.

English and Anglicisation

Most Burmese can understand English, although they may not use it very fluently. Having been an English colony for a long time, lots of older Burmese will intersperse English words and phrases in their speech. Many English words, such as "car", "bus", "telephone", "television", "doctor" and "film", have become part of the Burmese language. This is because Burmese requires a long string of descriptive words, whereas English is more concise. For example, the word "diary" in Burmese is literally translated as "daily record", "dentist" is a "doctor concerned with teeth" and "TV" is "a picture seen and sound heard". This makes the translated word very long and more like a definition.

English was once taught from kindergarten through to university level. Then in the 1960s there was a switch to Burmese as the medium of instruction and English was taught only from the fifth standard when children reached 11 or 12 years of age. The result of this policy was that proficiency in Burmese was very high while standards of English were very low. It was then that Burmese educational institutions lost their former international standing. However, since the late 1980s, English has once again been taught from kindergarten level.

Nevertheless, a whole generation of Burmese children have grown up without having learnt much English. This very inadequacy has led to a remarkable interest in learning the language, as can be seen from newspaper advertisements for English conversation and tuition classes. English-Burmese dictionaries, phrase books and glossaries are also very popular but are heftily priced.

Younger people are very eager to speak English and will love to practise on you if they can. With them, there is none of the feeling of using the "language of a slave colony" which English was generally thought to be by the older generation. The young consider it the language of business and of the world, and realise its importance in international dealings. They do not care so much about speaking with the correct English accent that those who lived through colonial times were so conscious of. The latter, in fact, would be very likely to sneer at mispronunciation and there are still a number of such people who feel they have to speak with an English accent to show their "class". In the same way, those who speak Burmese with a broad local accent are said to have a *nga-pi* accent, meaning literally a "fish paste accent". Fish paste is a staple of the Burmese diet and has a very strong smell, so the term is entirely derogatory.

Stresses

Stresses are the biggest problem for the Burmese when speaking English. For example, many will pronounce "vegetables" with stress on "tables". A common pronunciation of "boy" is "bwy" and "oil" sounds a bit like "wine". The "er" sound is pronounced with an open "ah", so "Burmese" is usually "Barmese", "fur" is "far, and so on. Moreover, the letters F, V, Q and X do not have equivalent sounds in Burmese. Thus the word "film" is pronounced "hpalin", "TV" sounds more like "TB" and "cubes" like "tubes".

Some English words have been rendered into Burmese sounds and when they are put back into English become something else entirely. For example, the typical shirt worn by Burmese men has a collar that is upright, rather like a Chinese collar. This is called a "stiff collar", but with a Burmese accent it sounds something like "sa tit-kawla". When rendered back into English many consequently write it as "stick collar"!

Burmese

Burmese is a monosyllabic language and a single sound can mean entirely different things depending on the context. Thus, one can use the language in many ways to make insults or innuendos and still get away with it by saying that the meaning was misconstrued.

Because of this the Burmese characteristically spend of lot of time interpreting various speeches and things that others have said to them. In fact, this pastime has become obsessive with some people, so that even a simple question like, "Is so-and-so still working in this organisation?" can be interpreted as meaning, "This person should not be working here anymore," a suggestion which could result in his transfer to another job!

Old Burmese has a flowery style, while modern Burmese is more to the point. Since the socialist period the language has become loaded with political expressions and slogans, as can be seen from a quick glance at newspapers. (For business language, turn to Chapter Eight.)

Will I Need to Learn Burmese?

The visitor does not need to learn to speak Burmese to get by in Burma as most understand basic English. Learning Burmese can be a tricky business as the different tones are hard to master.

At present there are no classes in Burmese on offer, except to serious scholars at the Foreign Language Institute.

Phrases and short sentences may be memorised for social purposes but mastering the tones will take some time. You can practise on your domestic staff who will be happy to teach you basic phrases.

At first, the writing will look very confusing because the round shapes seem to have little variation. For example the letter *nga* looks like the letter C, while the number one looks like a reversed C with the opening on the left. Zero and the letter *wa* are represented by the same character, O.

Be careful that, for a joke, some people don't teach you swear words, telling you that the phrase means "good morning" or "thank you". A Chinese friend learnt the greeting *nwa gyi*, thinking that he was saying "hello". In fact he was calling out, "Big cow"!

"Yes" can mean "No"

Because a negative answer involves a loss of face for the parties concerned, the usual answer to any question will be "yes". You will have to consider the meaning of any "yes" with some care as it can really mean "no". This process is very annoying for Westerners who are usually used to more direct methods of communication.

Even when speaking English, "yes" will be the usual answer. You have to learn to be patient and not take every "yes" at its face value.

Insults

As far as insults go, being compared to a dog is the worst. An S.O.B. label will also anger the person to whom it is attached because it insults his mother more than himself.

Swearwords are used by the less educated and less refined, and are likened to "fishmonger's talk".

The ultimate gesture of contempt is spitting, either really doing it or just symbolically making the sound "twee". Old-fashioned parents may do it when their children do something which they really disapprove of or when there's a quarrel and a hot exchange of words.

Body Language

In Burma, the most acceptable body language seems to be one of self-effacement, modesty and self-control. Loud, boastful behaviour is frowned upon.

Public shows of affection are also uncommon. At one time it was even taboo for a woman to be seen out in public with a man who was not her husband. Even now it is not common to see couples walking hand-in-hand or embracing in streets. However, girls and women will frequently be seen holding hands and linking arms in public.

Respect to elders is always heavily stressed in traditional families and this is reflected through body language. Young girls and boys are taught to walk lightly and not stamp around when they walk near grandparents and other elders. They are also expected to run errands for them, such as getting their spectacles, grinding *thanaka* on the grinding stone for grandma to use after her bath (see page 107), getting water for grandfather and so on.

Obedience is required more than anything else. Talking back and being rebellious are rarely tolerated. Young boys and girls must bow slightly when they walk past elders and they must never sit on a level which is above their heads. When handing objects to them they should use the right hand, supported by the left hand at the elbow. One should also never pass objects over superiors' heads.

At night it is usual to pay respects to grandparents and parents by doing the gesture of obeisance known as *kadawt*. It is sometimes called the *kow tow*, although this has a meaning of obsequiousness attached to it. In this gesture the children kneel on the floor in front of seated elders and bow to the ground with their hands held in front of the chest, palms together. This gesture is used to offer thanks, to show respect and to ask forgiveness for any inadvertent disrespect they may have shown.

This same gesture is used when praying and when greeting or offering things to monks. It is also included in special school ceremonies, usually held before exams or at the end of term, to thank and pay respect to teachers.

Slapping the face is the biggest insult to the Burmese. Perhaps this is why the Japanese were not easily forgiven for their habit of slapping the faces of local people during their occupation. Similarly, the Burmese cannot understand how the Japanese could slap their children's faces when disciplining them.

Lefthandedness

In earlier times, lefthandedness was discouraged and "southpaws" were forced to use the right hand for eating and writing. The left hand is only used for cleaning the backside after a visit to the toilet, so it is not used to pass objects to others, especially to elders, honoured guests or monks and nuns.

Nowadays lefthanded children do not have such a hard time, although they may invite comment whenever they eat or write.

Smiles

The Burmese are always smiling; little short laughs are added to every sentence, especially when they feel shy or embarrassed, or are uncertain about how to react in difficult situations. Even on sad occasions they may still smile and laugh. This is because they do not wish to inflict their grief upon you or make a nuisance of themselves if they can help it. They will be self-controlled and will remain the gracious host should you call on them during a bereavement.

In situations involving foreigners, they may be particularly uncertain of themselves as they are generally not used to dealing with outsiders. Because they cannot articulate feelings and thoughts effectively, they may just fill up the spaces in time with smiles. Particularly if they feel their English is not good enough, they will be silent but smiling. Smiles can mean that the person is embarrassed, angry, sad or feeling very *ah-nar-de*. Often they can simply mean "hello". Smiles can be bright, rueful, bitter or shy, and one should learn how to differentiate between them.

HUMOUR

Burmese are naturally fun-loving and even in extremely hard times or crises they can still find something to laugh about. Jokes of a political nature have been in abundance in recent times. This appears to be the common way of getting rid of any frustrations felt about the establishment.

A famous comedian, Zarganar (whose name means "tweezers"), has been in jail for a long time because of his brilliant jokes and skits at the expense of the government. One of the most famous concerns a government official who visited him in prison with the news that he would be released if he stopped telling jokes about the government. The story goes that Zarganar was challenged by the official to make up a joke on the spot. In reply he asked for a newspaper, a plastic mug and a bucket of water. Holding the newspaper in one hand, he pushed the floating mug down into the water with the other, cursing, "This stupid mug just keeps on reappearing." The joke was that it was the official's face on the front page of the newspaper!

Anecdotes and storytelling are common ways of relieving boredom and frustration. Sitting around a teapot and drinking endless cups of tea while exchanges take place is a common leisure pursuit. Contrary to the *machismo* of other cultures, jokes do not normally revolve around sexual conquests or exploits.

Since the Burmese language is monosyllabic, it lends itself easily to puns and spoonerisms. Puns are the most common jokes since most words have two or three meanings. For example, two people make a bet that one will jump off a balcony in the event of losing the bet. What he will really do is take a chair onto the balcony and lower it, since the words for "jump" and "chair" are the same.

Similarly the word for "teeth" and "go" are the same, so it's common to hear the lament that visits to dentists are never ending, because one has to "go" again and again.

Jokes about inflation and the standard of living in Burma are also popular. One famous anecdote tells of a visitor to Burma who first made to a phone call to London and then one to hell. When he asked the operator how much they cost, the call to hell was much cheaper than the one to London. He couldn't understand this logic until the operator explained that the call to hell was classified as a local call.

Similarly, when there were rumours about Burma joining the Asean nations, people said that the country would have to change its name to "Burmasia" to be in line with countries like Malaysia and Indonesia. The joke was that "Burmasia" sounds like *bar-may-sha* , a phrase which literally means "whatever you want is expensive and cannot be found".

Cartoons are also very clever in their comments on current times. Many make digs at the extortionate price of common food and groceries or the characteristic of Burmese women to compete with each other, similar to the Western idea of "keeping up with the Joneses".

Spoonerisms

Government and civil service personnel are sent to a place called Phaunggyi where there is a school for indoctrination and military training, an experience so universally dreaded that many will even threaten resignation to avoid being sent there. When they return, the course participant is said to have graduated from *Phaunggyi-hsinn* which can be turned around to *phin gyi saung,* meaning a "big twisted backside"!

Similarly, the spoonerism for the term *hpon-tin* (meaning "full of dust") is *hpin ton*, a "trembling or jerking backside".

Some words in English sound like bad words in Burmese (although this must be true in every language). Thus, Burmese may swear and then pretend that they were speaking English.

Teasing

Teasing is actually a sign of affection although some inveterate teasers can tease till their victims cry. However, teasing generally implies intimacy and closeness. Friends like to tease each other over mistakes, clumsiness, childhood escapades or about boyfriends or girlfriends.

You may also be teased if your Burmese friends like you and if you are close to them. You should take it as a compliment which shows their affection for you rather than as an insult. There is usually no malice behind their teases. If there was, they would generally do it behind your back!

DRESS

Burma is one of the few Asian countries left in Southeast Asia where local people still continue to dress in traditional costume. Most neighbouring countries have forsaken traditional dress for western skirts and trousers, wearing traditional outfits only for special occasions and ceremonies.

For ladies, traditional dress consists of a sarong, or *longyi*, and a short waist-length blouse. The sarong is made of material stitched in a circular fashion, with a black cloth for a waist band. It is folded in front to form a deep pleat and tucked in at the side, either right or left. Traditionally they were worn ankle-length but now are calf-length or shorter. The traditional blouse has an overlapping front, rather like an intern's uniform, and this flap is buttoned up at the side.

For the men, the sarong is usually decorated with checks or stripes, never with the flowers or solid colours that the women wear. The men will wear the sarong with an ordinary western-style shirt or one with a small upright collar similar to the Chinese. Men always tie their sarong in a knot in front.

The sarong is a practical garment that serves many purposes. When bathing at the public well, women can pull it over their breasts and bathe; it can be turned around if dirtied or stained; it can be used to wipe a sweaty face; it makes sitting down on the floor very easy when paying respects to monks and elders; and it can be loosened after a big meal or to cool one's legs on a hot day. Perhaps best of all, the sarong allows one to get slim or grow stout without the need for alteration.

On formal occasions and at weddings, the head gear for men is a kind of hat made of silk with a loose flap at the side. Bridegrooms will also wear this on their wedding day. Women need to wear a long net shawl over their shoulders on formal occasions. In rural areas, men and women will cover their heads with towels in the early mornings and also when carrying baskets and other objects on their heads.

Leather or velvet slippers with thongs are usually worn, although nowadays sandals and shoes are particularly popular with fashionable singers and actresses. (Shoes are actually called "ladyshoes", probably a corruption of "ladies shoes".) Men used to wear shoes and socks up to the 1960s but the dire lack of consumer goods since then has meant they now wear utilitarian rubber slippers for everyday and velvet slippers for better occasions.

Each of the ethnic groups has its own colourful costumes for the men and women. Usually they wear trousers or leggings as they live in the hills and mountains where the climate can be very cold at times. Thick cotton or wool materials are used and black is usually the dominant colour.

The major disadvantage with Burmese traditional costume is that the sarong can soon come loose and has to be retied after any vigorous movement. A number of visitors have reported getting a shock to see women and men retying their sarongs in public. Women will usually go to any available corner or face a wall to retie their sarong. It does tend to look like the beginning of a strip tease!

In countries neighbouring Burma, the sarong has come to have some class associations; only servants, maids and the lower income classes continue to wear them. This is not the case in Burma. Burmese women will probably never totally give up wearing the *longyi*, although, with the inevitable onslaught of Western ways, it may be that more fashionable designs and tailored sarongs will become popular, after the fashion of the Western-style skirts.

Indeed, for many years now, actresses and singers have worn new styles invented by dressmakers. If the majority of women have not followed their lead it is mostly because of the cost, not a lack of desire to be fashionable. Singers and actresses set the style by wearing stockings, jeans, boots and clothes resembling Western dresses on stage.

Many young girls do not own a proper Burmese blouse and merely wear a T-shirt or Western-style blouse over their sarong. A visiting friend once described it as a "half-dressed look". One of the reasons for preferring T-shirts to traditional tops is because each blouse has to be tailor-made and it is far less costly and troublesome to wear a T-shirt. Also good materials are generally very expensive as they can only be obtained on the black market. For the average clerical worker a yard of lace material for a blouse would be a month or two's wages (roughly K1000 or more).

Many young men own blue denim jeans which they wear when travelling. Men who wear trousers are somehow less frowned upon than women who wear shorts, skirts or dresses. Burmese women themselves prefer to wear trousers than dresses as they are conservative about exposing their legs. Even expatriate Burmese women will continue to wear their traditional clothes as far as the climate will allow or at least in the house.

Make-up

Burmese women are often photographed for the *thanaka* they wear on their cheeks. *Thanaka* is obtained from the bark of a small tree by grinding it on a circular grinding stone with a few drops of water. The pale yellow paste that is formed is used by females of all ages on the face, arms and legs. The *thanaka* liquid, when it dries on the skin, helps to control oiliness and has a light fragrance which Burmese women like very much.

Rice transplanting or harvesting workers will wear thick *thanaka* on their cheeks and nose to prevent sunburn. In the cold season a cream would be applied as a base to prevent the skin from drying out.

Modern girls wear eye make-up, rouge and foundation, but *thanaka* is traditional and may still be worn mixed with cosmetics. Even expatriates as far away as London and Australia have the traditional *thanaka kyauk pyin* (grinding stone). This is so heavy that one wonders how it could be transported overseas, probably by boat through the kind services of a courier friend (see Chapter Seven).

Older women do not go to extremes to look young as age is not something Burmese women try to hide. Probably the one vanity that older Burmese women will indulge in is to dye their hair black. This may be because the traditional hairstyle for women (hair pulled back and coiled in a bun) is a very severe style and black hair makes it look much better. Short hair is only for children, those who have been very ill or ladies of Chinese descent who like to perm their hair no matter what their age. Old age is inevitable according to Buddhist teaching, so, in Burmese eyes, old women wearing make-up are considered undignified or not "decent-looking".

A traditional shampoo, obtained from the bark of a vine called *tayaw* and mixed with some seeds of *kin pun* pods, is also commonly used. This gooey substance keeps the hair smooth and the scalp cool. Coconut oil may be used daily or weekly to keep the scalp oiled and prevent dry hair.

LEISURE

While earning a living seems to preoccupy most Burmese during the current economic troubles, they still find time to relax, to entertain and be entertained.

The TV and video are popular choices for those who have them but the Burmese, being a literate people, also love to read. Material may vary from news digests to translations of the latest Jackie Collins novel, but the vast majority of books and magazines will be borrowed because of the price and limited availability of any kind of literature in Burma.

More artistic pastimes like painting, sculpture and photography are increasing in popularity and have large followings of enthusiasts in the major towns. Many young artists hold exhibitions in Rangoon and Mandalay, and photography competitions are regularly held, entries coming from all over the country.

As far as the ethnic arts and crafts are concerned, one should remember that for the majority of Burmese these are hardly "hobbies" but rather livelihoods that have been carried out by families for generations. The Burmese would not choose such handicrafts as pottery, weaving and lacquer work as a hobby.

Sports

Of the spectator sports, the best-loved is soccer. Soccer matches are usually rowdy and often require police security. Of course, soccer is also one of the most commonly played games in Burma as almost any ball will do and makeshift goal posts are easy to devise. Sports like golf and tennis are for the well-to-do as they are expensive to play.

December is usually designated the month for sports because it is cool then. Marathons, walkathons and other events in which lots of people can take part are organised in Rangoon and the larger towns.

Burma's most famous traditional sport is *chinlone*. This is played with a cane ball by men (and now women) standing in a circle and trying to keep the ball in the air, using almost any part of the body except the hands. It is very entertaining to watch and play, and you can see it being played on the streets, open spaces and even in office compounds after work.

The Burmese also have their own style of boxing. If you go to watch a match, you may find this rather violent as the boxers are allowed to use any part of the body to fight with and the winner is the first participant to draw substantial quantities of blood. A boxer is allowed to wipe away blood three times before being declared the loser. However, it is a popular sport in Burma and famous boxers tour the towns, especially during the pagoda festivals. The matches are even given orchestral accompaniment!

Thaing is the Burmese martial art. It is a form of self-defence practised generally by enthusiasts, although it has been popularised in the movies just like Chinese *kung-fu*. Sometimes *thaing* players use long swords called *dah*.

Music and Dancing

The Burmese love to watch *pwe*, the dances and plays usually performed at festivals and celebrations. Most of these are performed in large bamboo-covered tents, with the audience sitting on the floor on mats (these are bought, just like seats at the cinema). Often the *pwe* start in the late evening and continue until the early hours of the morning. It is common for the audience to eat, drink, chat, smoke and doze off throughout the performance.

The plays are usually adaptations of the *Jataka*, a collection of stories about the Buddha's previous existences, especially as animals like the King of the Monkeys or the King of the Lions. The performers are troupes which have specialised in performance for generations. One of the most famous is the Shwe Mann Tin Maung Troupe, now in its third or fourth generation.

Sometimes the *pwe* are held in the open and it can get cold towards dawn. The older folk will tie towels around their heads and shoulders, like a shawl. Some are so addicted to these performances that they watch continuously for several nights and end up with red eyes from lack of sleep.

Musical performances are seldom held in their own right as they are in the West. The Burmese seem to prefer combinations of dancing and singing, although concerts may be seen on TV. Performances include stage shows in which pop stars sing modern Burmese songs, usually Western hits with Burmese lyrics.

Chapter Five

VISITING AND ENTERTAINING

FEASTS (SOON-KYWAY)

The most common type of entertaining in Burma is feasting, the meals offered to monks and laymen for religious reasons. In addition to the food, other gifts like dried provisions, robes, slippers and medicines are offered. The objective is to gain merit in the religious sense and the greater the number of people fed, the greater the merit. Not surprising, then, that people in rural areas get into debt over feasts like these!

At this type of feast, which can be held either in a monastery or at home, the guest monks will first recite prayers and give blessings.

After this they are offered a meal in return, usually as sumptuous as the donor can afford. Once the monks have been served the guests may be seen to.

Because monks keep the Ten Precepts, one of which prohibits eating after noon, these feasts are either held at dawn (anytime between 4 and 6 a.m.) or in the late morning (about 10 or 11 a.m.). The feast should not take place too close to 12 o'clock as that would not give the monks enough time to finish their meal.

This type of feast is offered especially on birthdays, at funerals, for novitiation ceremonies and on the anniversaries of deaths. Newly-weds may also hold one to gain merit together and sometimes they are offered as thanks for getting that new job, receiving a windfall or bringing home one's first pay-packet.

Other types of communal feasting take place at birthday parties, usually for children, and gatherings of close friends at different homes on the weekends.

In Rangoon, Mandalay or the larger towns, foreign visitors are likely at some time to be invited for either tea at 3 or 4 p.m. or an evening dinner at around 7 p.m. If you are invited to lunch it is around noon, somewhat early by Western standards. So, if you are a late sleeper you should have only a light breakfast. Burmese usually offer guests a really hearty meal and would be disappointed if you did not do justice to it.

Invitations to Feasts

In rural areas you could be invited to a novitiation ceremony and feast where you can see the traditional dress and customs of the whole ceremony, from beginning to end.

Burmese usually invite whole families to a feast. Of course, not everyone has to go, but it is part of the duty of the host and hostess to invite everyone they possibly can, including extended families - the norm in Burma. However, usually *ah-nar-hmu* (the feeling of not wishing to cause inconvenience or impose) will take control and only a few representative members of a family will turn up at the feast.

The reason that Burmese invite "everyone" is also the result of *ah-nar-hmu*, as to leave anyone out would be a great loss of face. Actually, as long as there is no enmity between the two parties, there is no real reason to leave anyone out and not to invite a person is tantamount to meaning that there is no more friendly feeling left. On the part of host and hostess, the whole purpose of a feast is to feed and provide for as many as possible.

On the practical side, Burmese food is never prepared for a fixed number of servings but is rather on the lavish side, to accommodate as many guests as one has invited without the embarrassment of food suddenly running out. The feast does not comprise a great variety of dishes but is made up of large quantities of four or five foods served by a large number of helpers. The dishes are cooked earlier, sometimes even the night before, and are kept covered in an oil base and gravy to prevent them drying out and spoiling.

Children

Children, however small they may be, are never a considered a hindrance but are generally adored. They are always included in invitations and you can be sure your hostess will enjoy having them, trying to entertain them and exclaiming over them (especially Caucasian children who seem like dolls with their blond hair or blue eyes). Try not to get annoyed if everyone tries to caress your child or baby because of their unusual looks.

INTRODUCTIONS

Among Burmese, introductions are seldom made. At any gathering the conversation tends to be general and not much will be revealed about the people. This does not imply a lack of curiosity, as once one can get hold of someone who knows another you can be sure that he will be asked all sorts of questions to fill in the missing information. The real introduction and all relevant details about background, parents, children, scandals, prominent relatives and past history will be revealed only after a person has left and the remaining guests asked, "Who was that?"

When meeting foreigners, however, introductions are usually made. It is a custom now to exchange namecards if you carry them.

Get Names Right

Considering the difficulty of Burmese names, which we have already discussed in Chapter Four, it is best to try and concentrate on remembering a person by at least one of his names. Although Burmese will often address each other using full names, as a foreigner you will be excused for sticking to just one.

The Burmese are aware of the difficulties and will be likely to tell you what they wish to be called. For example, if you are introduced to someone named U Khin Maung Win, he may say, "Please call me Win", even though all his Burmese friends must call him by the complete name together with its honorific prefix. It is better not to call him Khin or Maung; Khin is a girl's name when it stands alone, while Maung is a common name, used, for instance, by his wife.

Personal Particulars

When meeting foreigners it is quite common for Burmese to ply them with questions about age, marital status, children, occupation, salary and other questions which Westerners would consider intolerably intrusive. However, Burmese are generally easy-going and would volunteer such information about themselves to show friendliness. They do not consider such questioning an invasion of privacy at all when dealing with outsiders.

If the Burmese see a man and woman who live together it is assumed they are married and they might be very puzzled when one of them turns up again with another partner. You could say they are naive. Even if you are married, don't be surprised if they express some shock or dismay that you don't have children. In Burmese reasoning, it is incomprehensible not to want a child, unless, of course, there is something wrong with you or you have too many already!

Information about age and rank is important to the Burmese so that they may correctly address each other and not offend. Burmese do not feel any need to hide their age and this usually goes for women too. You will undoubtedly be asked how old you are and your frank answer will be appreciated. However, they would be puzzled by a snub and if you really do not wish to reply you could just say, "I'm old enough to be..." or "I'm still a baby." Such friendly answers reveal nothing but are not as offensive as a refusal and you would not be pressed further. It is important to keep your good humour and not to take offence where none is meant. Burmese genuinely find it hard to guess the age of Caucasians.

On the other hand, Burmese may increase or decrease their age for various reasons. Increasing it is usually for the purpose of enrolling in school earlier and thereby taking important examinations earlier. Decreasing is for deferring retirement. You may ask how this can be possible? Generally it's due to poor records, offices being frequently relocated, forgeries undetected, bribes acceptable and files eaten by termites or simply lost!

Compliments

As with other Asian cultures, compliments are usually hard for Burmese to handle; they are inclined to be more embarrassed than flattered since they are brought up to be modest. The usual reply might just be a shy smile rather than a straight-faced "thank you". Paying a compliment to a woman is even more likely to receive a silent non-response.

Among Burmese it is seldom that one would compliment a person on his or her clothes. The classic good-humoured reply to a compliment like "How nice you look," might be, "Oh, you know, I haven't even taken a bath yet!" (implying, "I would look even better after a bath," or "I look this good even before a bath.").

To a compliment like, "What a pretty blouse!" the reply might be,

"That's because *I'm* wearing it" or "Is it just the blouse that looks great? Aren't you going to compliment the wearer?" This is a typically coy answer. The point is, Burmese are uncomfortable with compliments.

Sincere, simple statements are better than lavish and effusive compliments which your local friends will not know how to take.

SEATING AT MEALS

Seating at Burmese meals is never important because the typical table is round; unless your host is familiar with Western customs, he will probably not seat you and you may have to choose for yourself.

In typical village homes, the table is low and round and you sit either on small stools or on mats. In urban homes, Western-style tables and chairs are more common. At a square or oblong table the head of the family or the most senior member will sit at the head of the table. The mother will sit beside the father and serve him food first. If there are other older people present, such as grandfather or grandmother they must be served first. If the oldest or most senior person is not present, a small portion of food is spooned up and then put back in the dish as a gesture that the person has been remembered.

Younger people are not supposed to take their first bite or taste until the elders have been served.

This is not strictly followed in every family. For example, very young children may be fed first at mealtimes. Generally, however, women tend to eat last at any meal since they are often busy with serving up the food and refilling dishes. Menfolk are pampered; they have to be served with water and anything else their tastebuds suddenly tell them should be added to the meal.

In homes where there are servants, they will perform these serving tasks. But, when entertaining guests, it is usual for the womenfolk (the mother and daughters) to eat last as they serve guests and the men.

What to Do and Say

A typical Burmese meal will have all the dishes spread out and is not served in courses. Do not be surprised if the hostess and children do not join you. They may prefer to stand around and serve you, fan you with a palm fan (to keep occasional flies away) and see to your other needs.

Portions of each dish are taken and placed next to the rice which is in the centre of the plate. Usually a fork and spoon are used. Use the spoon to eat the rice, meat and vegetable dishes. For soups, a Chinese spoon, shaped with the handle sloping upwards is usually provided. If not, you must use the same spoon for the soup.

A small, shallow saucer beside your plate is for placing any bones on.

Burmese normally use their fingers to eat, although they do not do so when they have foreign visitors. Because of the habit, many dining rooms have a small sink or basin in one corner for the purpose of washing hands and mouth after a meal.

Being belittled for eating with fingers, as if it was a barbarous habit, had one friend asking his tormentor, "So, do you eat with your feet?" This is a sensitive issue and it is best not to ask about it unless you yourself wish to try it.

There is a way to eat neatly with the fingers: mix enough rice for a mouthful with some meat or gravy into a rough ball. Then, draw the fingers into a bud and pop the food into your mouth. It is a natural way to eat and many Burmese dislike using forks and spoons, which they may be clumsy with. If they have to, they prefer to use just the spoon and not the fork.

Conversation will tend to be minimal as Burmese are not great conversationalists over dinner. The objective in eating is to enjoy the food. Western dining, with its leisurely style of savouring food and enjoying dining room conversation, is not the norm here. The talk is more lively over a pot of tea and snacks rather than at dinner. Talking business over dinner at someone's home is also considered rather bad taste, especially if other guests or the hostess do not know much about business or do not know the language fluently.

One should ask questions about the food, the way dishes are prepared and cooked, and about ingredients. Questions about ceremonies and other general topics are also suitable as your host and hostess will usually enjoy answering them.

FOOD

Burmese food consists largely of oil-based curries, salads with fresh or boiled vegetables, various types of salted fish recipes and soups, all of which are eaten with rice. Herbs are nearly always used, the common ones being ginger, turmeric, garlic, chilli, lemon grass and coriander.

Burmese food has not seen much refinement over the years as Burma has been closed for so long. There has not been much room or opportunity for improvement. For one thing the quality and variety of ingredients has been desperately lacking which limits good cuisine. It is also rather difficult to obtain good fare at restaurants simply because there have not been that many tourists who would be interested in local food. For the most part Burmese food remains simple and dishes are usually ungarnished in any way.

Burmese food is best sampled in Burmese homes. Good Burmese cuisine is rather hard to find, even more so in a typical Burmese setting. Several large cities around the world have Burmese restaurants (good ones can be found in London, Boston and Bangkok) but in Burma itself they are ironically hard to find, except in the big towns like Rangoon and Mandalay. Even then, these are rarely top-notch restaurants.

Preparations for Burmese food take a long time and cooking has to be done in advance, unlike Chinese food which is usually cooked upon order. This may also be a reason for the reluctance of entrepreneurs to invest in Burmese cuisine. With an uncertain clientele anyway, the risk of unsold food is perhaps too great.

There are places where delicious Burmese food is dished out of big pots and served up fresh and hot, but generally the setting is rather poor as no one has the time or money to spare a thought on decor.

As Burma opens up, it is expected that with demand there will

Women selling freshwater fish which is much used in Burmese cuisine.

119

soon be much more competition in serving authentic Burmese cuisine. Until then try to wangle an invitation from your Burmese hosts!

The Art of Home Cooking

Burmese food is generally bought and cooked fresh, and the older generation particularly prefer shopping to be done every morning. Daily markets selling fresh food are usually nearby. This is perhaps because storage is a problem in Burma's heat and the soaring temperatures at certain times of the year can cause some food to become stale in a matter of hours, making it safer to throw old food away. Even where there are refrigerators, many do not keep cooked foods in them but only water bottles! Storage in cat safes is the usual method of preserving food and keeping it away from insects and flies.

The cat safe is a small cupboard with doors and sides made of mesh. It has four legs which stand in small earthen bowls of water to prevent ants from climbing up.

Burmese women cook without written recipes and the only way to really learn from them is to watch and measure with your eyes the quantities of ingredients, herbs and spices. Most Burmese women learn this way, by watching mothers, aunts and friends.

The lack of specific measuring should not be mistaken for a slap-dash style of cooking. Burmese cooks are very precise and "timing" is essential. In fact, one of my favourite aunts will begin cooking and then trot off to the garden to practise her golf-putting, returning at specific intervals to stir the pot and add herbs - so fine is her sense of timing!

Burmese women love to cook for large gatherings; in fact a good cook must be one who can reproduce the same culinary delights regardless of the size of the pot. This requires great skill as cooking in large proportions can easily go wrong: the fire may not be hot enough, the pot not deep enough, the ingredients not in proportion etc.

Cooking methods do not differ much between the villages and towns, although the kitchen, utensils and fuels might vary. In the villages, wood fires are most common and pots are either earthenware (for sour or slow-cooking dishes) or aluminium coated with mud and soot to keep the metal from turning black. In the towns, electrical appliances and even microwaves are used only by the more affluent but nearly every home will have a rice-cooker.

A Typical Burmese Meal

Home-cooked Burmese meals can be very elaborate. A complete meal traditionally includes a main dish of meat or fish, a vegetable dish, dips or sauces to eat with blanched or pickled vegetables and a soup. It could also include side dishes such as fried dried shrimps known as *balachaung* and a second or third vegetable dish.

The main meat or fish dish will usually be in the form of a curry with an oil base. The spices, onions and garlic are pounded in a stone mortar with a pestle (found in every Burmese home) and then cooked in oil before the meat or fish is added. While there is not much variety of meat, there are a lot of different types of freshwater fish which Burmese love to eat and actually prefer above meat.

There are also a large variety of vegetables, leaves, shoots and young fruits which can either be cultivated or obtained from the wild.

However, due to inflation most Burmese (especially in urban areas) are unable to afford such elaborate meals any more. Meat is very expensive and, if there is any at all, it is usually mixed with vegetables to make it go further. Even common meat substitutes like eggs, dried fish and beans have risen in price.

Indian and Chinese Influences

Being geographically situated between two great nations, India and China, it is inevitable that Burmese food should be influenced by Chinese and Indian cuisine. Indian spices are used in curries, as is Chinese soy sauce. Stir-frying and steaming methods are widely used and many Burmese stall owners will serve Indian or Chinese food.

Malay and Peranakan influences can be seen particularly in cakes and desserts where coconut flavouring, pandan leaves (screw pine) and rice flour bases have become common.

Burmese themselves will go to Chinese restaurants on special occasions and to entertain guests. It is not usual to go to Indian restaurants as they are now rarely found since the large exodus of Indians in the 1970s. However, Indian *briyani* made with chicken is very popular at feasts because it is a one-dish meal that is considered quite sumptuous in view of the price of meat.

Western Food

English food is very much appreciated, although more so by those who lived and worked during colonial times. It was possible to obtain good English roasts, mixed grills and soups in many hotels until about the late 1960s. After this they all died a natural death due to the lack of people to cook these meals, the lack of good ingredients and a lack of customers.

Traditional Dishes

Traditional dishes have many versions around the country. One of the most famous is *mohinga*, thin or flat rice noodles eaten with a fish-based soup. Other versions have different types of soups. A bean powder sauce or soup is often used in areas where good freshwater fish cannot be obtained easily and beans and pulses are abundant.

This dish is the favourite of all Burmese and they especially love to eat it early in the morning before going to work. When served piping hot with fresh crisps and sprinkled with chopped coriander, the smell really is enough to make your mouth water. It seems one can find it almost anywhere. Itinerant pedlars, with a pot hanging from one side of a yoke-like pole, and a small table and stools hanging from the other, will sell *mohinga* on the street. Alternatively you can try it in the larger shops. New *mohinga* shops turn up all the time and are heard of by word of mouth. Each of these will be tried out and a verdict passed. Burmese friends will gladly point you in the direction of their favourite shops and stalls, and if you ask nicely they may even cook it for you at home!

Mohinga is also served to monks and guests at feasts as it is a neat one-dish meal. It is cooked in large pots in the monastery grounds or at home by family and relatives, all of whom are expected to help out at feasts, if only to pour out plain tea for the helpers.

Another traditional dish which is often served at feasts and celebrations, is *ohno-khauk-swe*. This consists of Chinese-style yellow noodles and is eaten with chicken in a coconut-based sauce. It is very rich and filling and if eaten too often it tends to cause headaches, indigestion and high blood pressure as the coconut base is full of oil. Sometimes evaporated milk can be substituted. The Thais in Chiangmai, close to the Burmese border, make a similar dish called *khow swoy*.

As in all countries, each region has its specialities and food traditions. Mandalay is famous for its *mee-shay*, noodles which are mixed with pickled tofu, pork and preserved mustard. Maymyo specialises in a tofu salad; the Shan state has a dish called "Shan sour rice"; and Moulmein its durian and mango preserves. Due to its abundance of pineapples, Tavoy has pineapple rice, while the Dry

Zone's toddy palm is used to make a sugar called *jaggery* and an alcoholic wine called "toddy".

As for snacks, common ones include glutinous rice cakes wrapped

Small kiosks, like this one selling snacks, are everywhere.

in banana leaves and steamed; fritters of various vegetables; and *lepet* leaves marinated in oil with dried shrimps, garlic and sesame seeds.

Drinks

Plain water is usually drunk after food as most prefer not to drink it before and during meals.

Small road side shops will serve plain Burmese tea which is free. Wine would be served only at homes of Westernised Burmese as abstaining from intoxicating drinks is one of the Five Precepts all Buddhists are supposed to keep. For this reason, being a drinker is a bit of a stigma in Burma. Village drunks who lie about after drinking "toddy" are the only models with which drinkers are compared and there is no room for social drinking, except among Westernised Burmese.

At meals, mostly soups or green tea are taken as drinks. On special occasions local soft drinks known as "aerated waters" are served (all drinks come in bottles which are recycled as cans and paper cartons have not yet reached Burma). These drinks mostly consist of sugar, colouring and water with carbon added. They are of a low quality but are popular with children.

Pepsi cola has arrived in Burma but is in bottled form and is quite expensive for the average household budget.

Fruit

Burma has many different kinds of fruit because of the wide variations in climate between regions.

Tropical fruits like mangos come in many varieties and are available from March to July. The Burmese eat mangos in all shapes, sizes and stages of growth, from the small sweet ones to the large green ones which are still sour and used in salads.

From about June to October, jackfruit is available. There are two kinds of jackfruit, one with firm flesh and the other with a sweet, fibrous, slimy flesh. Other fruits that are abundant include guava, watermelon, rambutan, pomelo, bananas, plums, papaya, lychee, grapes and pineapples.

Temperate fruits like apples, oranges, tangerines and grapefruits come from the Shan plateau which means they are not readily available in all areas because of transport problems. Strawberries are also grown in the Shan state and Maymyo. Again, because they do not form a normal part of consumption patterns in the rest of the country, some Burmese believe that they actually grow on trees as they have never seen the plant!

When eating fruit in Burma there are a number of things you should be aware of. Firstly, with mangos do be careful not to eat too close to the stem as the sap can give you a very sore throat. The Burmese cut off the stem and put the whole fruit in water for some time so that the sap flows out.

A stain from a mangosteen is very difficult to remove and did you know that the number of calyxes on top of the fruit show how many segments there are inside?

Similarly, the stripes of a melon show where the seeds lie and if you cut along the lines you will be able to remove the seeds easily.

Custard apples, a fist-sized fruit with scaly skin and soft white flesh, contains many small seeds which you should be careful of around children. There are many stories of children and babies having to go to hospital after inserting seeds in noses and ears when playing.

It's B.Y.O. (Bring-Your-Own)

Food prices have gone up so much that most workers will carry their own food boxes to work and share them with colleagues.

Women workers will carry a small, oblong basket of cane or bamboo and put their food box and flask in it. In urban areas, buses will be crowded with women workers precariously hanging on to the strap or seat back with one arm and clinging to their lunch baskets with the other. The men, many of whom go to work on bikes, can be seen with their lunch boxes strapped to the carrier.

Most workers usually prefer to eat their own home-cooked food despite the trouble of having to prepare and cook it before coming to work. This is because canteen fare is usually of very low quality, not to mention the adulteration of food with additives, some of which are even toxic substitutes.

There have indeed been food scares in the past. This has included rumours about tissue paper being mixed with milk skin (the latter is used like cream to put in coffee or tea) and another about various toxic oils being mixed with edible oils.

What is certain is that you should be careful when consuming roadside food. It may look tasty but the preparation of it might be completely unhygienic. Dysentery and other intestinal diseases can be contracted from such food. The Burmese are more or less immune to many diseases through constant exposure but even expatriate Burmese have been known to fall ill when they visit their country again after an interval.

Rice, Please!

Most Burmese need to eat rice at every meal, from breakfast to dinner, to feel they have really eaten. Other types of starchy and filling food are not so popular. For example, cakes and cookies are only for special occasions. Bread is consumed mostly in urban areas and then only at breakfast or teatime.

The production of flour in the country is low and imports are relied on. This makes even inferior quality biscuits and cakes expensive.

Dairy products are also scarce because there are few local dairy industries or farms. For most, the breeding of cattle is not a potential livelihood because of cultural taboos concerning animals, especially cows. Nevertheless, it is said that the few milk suppliers that do exist can supply any number of homes - they just add water to the milk!

In any case, milk is hard to get and where you can get it, it is hard to say whether it is free of bacilli. Everyone who uses fresh milk has to boil it to ensure it is safe enough to drink.

On the whole, ice cream, cheese and butter are quite scarce. The Burmese have not acquired a taste for cheese but most like to eat ice cream and use butter on their bread, both of which were easy to obtain at one time. Local industries produce condensed milk and butter, but not enough by far. For milk and ice cream one goes to the Indian quarter of the towns.

Exotic Food and Delicacies

Burmese eat various kinds of exotic foods which you may never get to sample unless you ask, your host fearing to insult your tastebuds or table manners with the unfamiliar. They are again served at certain times of the year when they can be obtained.

For example, pickled tea leaves are a speciality served with fried peanuts, fried beans, garlic, dried prawns, sesame seeds and an oil dressing. Other delicacies include fried crickets, pickled bamboo shoots, pickled ferns, cooked field crabs, mice, snake, a type of larvae and fish innards.

On the markets, one sometimes comes across deer hooves hung up together with meat, purporting to be venison. Do not be taken-in by the hooves. They are probably not related in any way to the meat being sold!

Food Superstitions

In line with oriental tradition, the Burmese have many food superstitions, some of which may be based on fact, others on fiction.

Sour foods, for instance, should not be consumed at the same time as milk products; sugar must not be eaten with mangosteen; and watermelon with eggs.

The Burmese also believe in certain foods being either "heaty" or "cooling". Foods conducive to "heatiness" are chicken, bitter gourd, durian, mango, chocolate and ice. "Cooling" foods are pork, eggplant, dairy products and radish.

Pregnant ladies should avoid bananas if they do not wish to have an over-weight baby, while chilli is supposed to make the baby's hair sparse. Glutinous rice is said to make the placenta stick to the womb, and mushrooms and bamboo shoots can lead to unconsciousness in some new mothers. After delivery, mothers are supposed to take plenty of clear soups to produce more milk and eat turmeric to avoid wind.

For sufferers of coughs and those with injuries or wounds, the fumes of frying chilli are said to increase the pain and irritation. Fried foods, oranges and cold or icy food are also bad for coughs. For relief, one should take honey and lemon, and chew on betel leaves.

Food as a Status Symbol

The economic situation in Burma has rendered even the price of rice expensive in comparative terms. Many people have been reduced to consuming low quality rice, even when it's been full of weevils or grains, thankful they had rice at all. This is virtually unbelievable considering the fact that Burmese rice was once known for its quality and was therefore an important export.

Canned foods are all imported and consequently even more expensive than fresh food! Canned sardines, which were eaten as side dishes up to the 1960s and were considered cheap substitutes for meat, are now very expensive. The same is true for instant foods and canned meats.

As for seafood, while the rivers and waters around Burma offer considerable varieties, some fish are ironically unaffordable or not available. Large Burmese prawns or lobsters are sold mostly for export and are hardly seen in the markets. A very delicious fish called *nga-myinn* (butterfish) now sells for a price way beyond most people's budgets.

This has led to a situation where even some basic foods are now considered luxuries. When they can be afforded they will generally only be served on special occasions, when entertaining guests and offering meals to monks (although, these days, even monks have experienced difficulty getting food for their begging bowls on their morning alms rounds.) It has also served to add to the status implications associated with food in Burma.

The poor man's food is rice, fish paste or fish sauce (*nga-pi*) and a few vegetables, boiled or pickled.

Another food considered cheap and not suitable for guests is a sour chowder made of vegetables and fish or shrimps. Tamarind is often added to this to create the sour flavour. Actually it is a delicious dish but there seems to be some hesitation when serving it to guests, possibly because of the sour taste. Also it is watery rather than oily, oil being considered the most suitable ingredient for feasts and special occasions. One look at the common feast foods that are swimming in oil is enough to make cholesterol-conscious Westerners shudder! But to stint on oil is the same as not being generous towards the guest.

Foods that imply status are meat dishes, lobsters, expensive fish like *nga-tha-lauk* (hilsa), *nga-myinn* and *nga-pe* (a fish which is scraped and pounded with spices, then rolled into balls and fried - a truly arduous process). Vegetables are local asparagus and mushrooms, both of which are expensive because they can only be obtained during their limited seasons.

It would appear that guests are second only to monks when it comes to meals. Consequently you may find an array of different meats all lined up with only a few vegetables. This is because meat is expensive and rare, while vegetables are more common. Moreover, vegetables have not yet become the health food that they are in the west. Good quality rice and oil is essential for guests and monks.

Other Places to Eat

In Rangoon there are many places to eat. The majority of them are Chinese restaurants, all competing fiercely with each other. New restaurants are set up, go out of business and are taken over all the time.

Chinese restaurants are frequented by locals, especially if they are taking you out to dinner. Chinese food is considered the most luxurious type of food to offer to guests.

As mentioned earlier, Burmese food is best sampled in the homes of Burmese friends as really good Burmese restaurants with Burmese dances, songs and decor are hard to find.

Western cuisine is now only found in the larger hotels.

Rangoon boasts a large night market where all types of food are served at hawker-style stalls. However, eating here when you are not used to the food could give you a bad case of diarrhoea or, even worse, cholera. Burmese themselves may go with their own containers and bring food home to eat. You can also try this but you should be aware that such places are usually crowded and dingy, where dogs, mice and cats like to loiter.

Itinerant hawkers and pedlars are also found going through residential areas selling everything from boiled corn cobs, beans and ground nuts to fruit preserves and cakes. If you want to buy from them you have to walk to your gate and call them over. But you should be careful as they have been known to resort to petty theft, such as stealing flowers from your garden and walking off with your laundry when your back is turned. Be sure to keep the gate closed at all times so that it at least makes quick access difficult.

Mohinga is also sold by sellers who travel with a small table and little stools hanging on the end of a pole. They will find a place to set up their tables and stools, while customers (often regulars) gather round. Sellers also carry a small stove to keep the *mohinga* hot.

Other sellers offer a poor man's meat dish called *wet thar dok hto*. This consists of pig's innards boiled in spices and soya sauce till soft and delicious. The *dok hto* man will cut up the part which you wish to eat and put it on a thin bamboo stick. You can then dip your piece into a garlic and chilli sauce. *Dok hto* in fact means "speared with a stick." When you've finished eating you must hold up the sticks to be counted so that your bill can be calculated. Cheating by surrepti- tiously dropping your sticks on the ground can make your bill a bit

Most Burmese have their favourite tea shops and food stalls.

less! However, this type of food is probably best avoided by weak stomachs as the innards may cause worm infestations and the sauce is dipped into by one and all.

Tea houses are also very popular for snacks and tea or coffee. In Burma, tea and coffee are already mixed with milk and sugar (usually sweetened condensed milk). You can get black coffee or plain tea only if you ask specially for it. Snacks are usually fried spring rolls, meat buns (Chinese buns), sandwiches and small cakes.

Tea shops are usually quite pleasant places, with small gardens where you can sit and chat. They are perhaps more hygienic than most hawker stalls because properly cooked, hot food is available. Couples, students and retirees are the frequent customers, especially so in the outskirts of Rangoon. In town these places are filled with office workers taking a tea break and people making business deals, like selling a car or having goods cleared through customs.

Other food stalls are also available wherever there are markets, known locally as *zay* (bazaars). These markets sell fresh vegetables, meat, fish, dried provisions, cloth and flowers. They also have rows of tailors and miscellaneous goods stalls. It is a good experience to walk around the aisles just to get to know what types of goods are available. You do not have to buy, although every seller is sure to ask you, "What do you want?"

Catering businesses offer a useful service. They will bring a layered carrier containing about three local dishes and rice to wherever you wish to eat. However, this service is quite expensive nowadays. Fast foods have not arrived yet and, even if they do, it is possible that burgers will not be as popular as traditional food because of the beef taboo for many Burmese.

DRESS

For invitations to morning ceremonies, feasts and special occasions, casual wear is appropriate but not shorts and T-shirts. Ladies would be better to choose light summer dresses or sleeved blouses/shirts with flared skirts (in case you should have to sit on carpets at floor level). For men, a shirt and tie is advisable but not a full suit. If you should be invited to a ceremony being held at a monastery, women should be sure to wear a sleeved dress or blouse and longish skirts.

For evening, dinner dresses are fine as long as they are not revealing, low cut or strapless. Being covered up helps to avoid mosquito bites as well as frowns or stares from hosts. For men short-sleeved shirts and trousers are appropriate. It is better to avoid shorts although your host may say the dress code is casual.

GIFTS

When visiting a Burmese home for a meal it is good take along a gift to show your appreciation. Chocolates, cookies, fruits and sweets are all acceptable gifts.

As with funerals and other special occasions, flowers do not have great significance as a gift. Flower cultivation has not played much part in the agricultural scene in Burma. Herbs and medicinal plants are cultivated but flowers are sold as altar offerings or for women to put in their hair rather than to adorn living rooms.

Similarly, it is not advisable to give flowers to sick friends. Food items such as fruits, biscuits, cordials or various powdered drinks, like Horlicks and Sustagen, are more meaningful.

Consumer items are appreciated: toys and crayons for children; toiletries and cosmetics for the hostess; calendars and diaries at the start of the year; and ball pens and shirts for the host are all suitable since they are hard to obtain and usually beyond the average household budget.

Liquor and cigarettes can also be given if your host smokes and drinks alcohol. Even if he doesn't, selling these on the black market will give him a good return which he can use to buy something which he really needs. While smoking cigarettes is common amongst men, women will smoke cheroots, if at all. Drinking alcohol is less common because of the Buddhist Precepts and women very rarely do so. Only the more Westernised and well-travelled Burmese are likely to consume alcohol.

Giving items like luxury underwear, handmade dolls, rare cheeses and bath salts are unlikely to be appreciated since these items are not commonly used. It is essentials which are lacking in every day life.

Avoid giving used and secondhand articles; even though these may be useful to your hosts, their pride could be offended. If you wish to do so, it should be when you leave the country for good and are really clearing out your things. Enquire gently if any of your unwanted things could possibly be used by anyone.

Burmese would give their own cast-offs to less wealthy relatives living in the rural provinces, to nephews, nieces, grand children or domestic staff. Even then such hand-me-downs are not given as important gifts but only incidentally, or in addition to better presents.

Pieces of cloth for your hostess are also nice gifts, especially when you know her better and you are able to guess her taste in materials and patterns. General favourites with Burmese women are batik pieces (which are worn as *longyis*), Thai silk and cotton. For a Burmese blouse, one metre or just over a yard (91cm) is sufficient, while a *longyi* takes about two metres, depending on the size of the lady. All clothes are tailor-made, hence the interest in cloth rather than in clothes. Such presents are often shared by mothers and daughters.

It seems that buying cloth to make into *longyi* and blouses is a favourite activity for all Burmese women and the markets are full of cloth stalls selling colourful pieces. Even remnants are good enough and there are now remnant stalls where one has to crawl and crouch to get at pieces of cloth piled up all over the floor. This proves two things about life in Burma: firstly, it is possible to make money out of even poor materials and, secondly, that no matter how high inflation soars and incomes fall, Burmese women are still trying to look their best.

CASUAL VISITS

Making casual visits among friends is very common for Burmese who will drop by when they are in the neighbourhood and have the time. It is not usual for Burmese to make appointments for visiting homes of close friends. Appointments imply self-importance, something which any modest Burmese abhors. Phoning is possible but telephone calls in Rangoon require great patience. As the distance from one place to another is not very great anyway, it is usual to go on impulse.

Even if your friends happen to be in the middle of entertaining others, you will usually be graciously invited to join in. Whether you accept or not is up to you.

Being the Perfect Guest

The perfect guest needs to know when to arrive and when to leave. You may be forgiven for arriving late but a continual habit of it may

135

cause your host to dub you "the late Mr/Ms .....", a common name for late superiors to be called behind their backs.

Leaving too late is found annoying because it is likely to throw your host off schedule the next day. Do remember that Burmese generally sleep early and get up early. Thus, even though you may have a lot of time to kill, it is good to leave your host's home by about 10 or 10.30 p.m. Leaving after midnight will result in only a few hours of sleep for your hosts.

Indeed, there is a saying that "the late guest causes the host sleeplessness."

THE OVERNIGHT GUEST

Due to government restrictions on locals mixing with foreigners, it appears unlikely that you would get around to spending a few nights in your host's home. Your host would have to go to the trouble of reporting your presence to local authorities. So, though you may wish to sample how Burmese live, it is perhaps better not to stay overnight.

However, if you do manage it, here are some do's and don'ts:

- *Don't* wear outdoor shoes in the house. Even slippers should be taken off when you enter the altar room or bedrooms.
- *Do* offer to wash dishes; it does not matter that there are servants to do this. The offer will be appreciated.
- *Do* try to entertain the children. Take along the kids when you go out and give them little treats: children are nearly always hungry or thirsty. You will find that once you get over their initial shyness they will follow you around everywhere and you might find it hard to shake them off.
- *Don't* expect to be entertained during the day. The likelihood is that your host works hard and is busy. Either please yourself or fit in and help out with your host's daily jobs.
- *Do* let your host know in advance whether you have specific things you'd like to do or whether you expect them to take you to certain places.

- *Don't* stay out all day without letting them know what time to expect you back and whether they need to include you in their meal plans. It is usually taken for granted that you will be eating with the family and they may be offended if you keep changing your plans or don't make the effort to sample their hospitality.

The Host's Duties

Your hosts may tend to pamper you. This is the way they try to make you feel at home and show that your welfare is important to them. Sometimes they will go out of their way to make your stay pleasant and you may not have an inkling of it. For example, they may call on close friends to pull a few strings here and there to make things easy for you, and they may spend time and money arranging little luxuries which a Westerner may simply take for granted.

You may at times find their questions intrusive but this is because, unlike Western people, Burmese are on the whole an extrovert race. They do not feel much need for privacy and may not realise that you do. In fact, there's no specific word for privacy in the Burmese language.

When a guest is staying in one's house, the host's duties include not merely providing a place to stay or sleep, but also giving information on good buys and where they can be found, providing meals and accompanying the guest to places of interest.

Beds

Beds are made without the top sheet, although hotel beds would be made in the Western way. One sleeps on the sheet and, when chilly, a light blanket may be provided.

Feet must be washed before getting into the bed and wiped with special cloths provided. Do not wash your feet in the sink but use the stored water usually provided in the jars by the sink. You'll also find a small bowl which is used for pouring. If you wear socks or slippers there is no need to wash your feet.

Sleeping in the buff is not advisable as homes lack privacy. There are usually no doors, just curtains which keep the air circulating but afford no seclusion.

Laundry

You should take care of your own laundry, especially underwear, even if your host has servants to do it for you. All laundry is usually done by hand. Having to wash other people's undergarments may be offensive.

Do not wash panties and socks in the sink but use a small plastic bucket or basin, usually found in the bathroom. Don't be afraid to ask your host or somebody the same gender as yourself.

Try not to hang your underwear out on the front porch but dry it in the bathroom or back room, the place where the women folk hang their *longyi* to dry. Also do not dry them at head level or where the towels are hung because the Burmese consider the lower and upper parts of the body very differently. The upper is held sacred, especially the head and hair, while the lower is very inferior and considered unclean. Women's *longyi* are considered especially unclean.

Toilets and Baths

Western-style houses will have flush toilets as well as Asian-style squatting toilets. There is usually a water basin or pipe near the toilet for washing yourself after you have finished. Burmese, like other Asians, tend to use of lot of water and so toilets are usually very wet and slippery.

Mops are not used but local coconut leaf stems are made into brooms and used for swishing out excess water on the floor.

In the villages, toilets are separate from the house and often some distance away. One needs a torch or candle for going to the toilet at night. Open pits are common and the only way to overcome the stench is to close your nose or to smoke perhaps. Be careful about valuable things in your pockets. Try not to carry them into the toilet in case they fall into the pit, never again to be retrieved! Be sure to wear flat slippers or shoes to avoid slipping. Shorts and skirts are best so that you can bend your knees to squat. Paper or water may not be available so it is best to carry Wet Ones or your own roll of toilet paper when travelling through villages.

In such cases it is often best to simply do your business behind the bushes; all you have to do is to cough whenever you hear someone coming so that your presence in the vicinity is known! Do look out for insects and leeches; snakes are not very likely but you should still be careful. Take a stick along with you. Hopefully you will never have to look for bushes, but you never know.

Bathrooms will not have hot water-heaters, except in the urban areas and then not every house will have one. Most take cold baths and only on cold days will water be boiled, usually for children and old folk.

Burmese take baths at least twice a day, once in the morning before going out to work and once again when they come home in the evening. Because of the unpredictable supply of water it is usual to store it in barrels or tubs. Even where bathtubs are available they have to be used for storing water. Water is not scarce in Burma, except perhaps in the Dry Zone. It is because of poor housing and the lack of proper water management (you'll often see water being wasted from leaking pipes) that water is now scarce in the city. Long queues form in the summer at the water taps in each quarter of the city and fights will ensue over queue-jumping.

Burmese do not find showers cooling enough and they dislike soaking in bath tubs even if they have one. Most find the thought of soaking in one's own dirty water quite loathsome. They prefer to bathe by dipping a small bowl into a water jar and pouring it over their heads. Actually this is a wasteful way to bathe but the Burmese never seemed to have become accustomed to any other method. Burmese student-friends studying in London once gave their landlady quite a shock when she discovered water flowing from the bathroom and all

over the bedroom carpet!

Bathing nude is also relatively new for the Burmese and is called "Japanese bathing", perhaps because they discovered this way of bathing during the Japanese occupation. More commonly, Burmese bathe at public wells and tanks. Men fold up their sarong into the waist like shorts, while women would wrap theirs over their breasts.

ENTERTAINING YOUR BURMESE FRIENDS

Naturally, after you have been in Burma for some time and have made some Burmese friends, you may want to return their hospitality by entertaining them.

Home or Restaurant?

The question of where to entertain your guests arises when you are thinking of a dinner invitation. The majority of decent restaurants are Chinese so eating out is limiting.

Home cooking is better, especially if you have the domestic staff to do the work while you supervise. The fact that you have invited people to your home will be appreciated. Moreover, restaurants do not provide much privacy. Private rooms can be booked in advance but this could prove costly.

What to Serve

When planning the menu do remember that pork and beef are the most commonly avoided meats. Pork is not consumed by those who have a tradition of worshipping *nat* (spirits) and beef is avoided by those who are devout Buddhists because the cow is highly regarded (perhaps because its existence has always been essential in pulling the paddy ploughs). Some devout Buddhists may also abstain from eating any meat obtained from four-legged animals.

During Buddhist Lent, which roughly coincides with the rainy season, some Buddhists become vegetarians and abstain from eating meat, fish and eggs. Other Buddhists will abstain from eating meat on the day of the week on which they were born. Consequently, if you cannot check on the preferences of your Burmese guests it is always best to serve a variety of dishes

Because rice is a staple, most Burmese never feel they have really had a meal unless they eat it. They complain of hollow feelings, even after eating bread, but after rice they describe "a nice cool feeling in the chest/breast" (meaning the stomach). They also do not like to eat noodles very much unless it is rice noodles. Thus, it is a good idea to serve some ordinary white rice besides bread, rolls, pastries and potatoes.

Large portions of meat are seldom consumed. Whole pork chops or slabs of beef are difficult for them to handle as their meat is almost

141

always cooked with some vegetables. They tend to prefer fish, shrimps or prawns. Younger people may, however, consume more meat than older guests.

You should also be aware that for some Burmese certain types of food are just too "difficult to eat". These include:

• raw tomatoes - in Burmese cuisine tomatoes are usually cooked.

• avocado served as a soup - at a dinner party I once heard it described to be so bitter that it could barely be swallowed. The guest speaking hardly knew what to do after taking a mouthful! Ripe avocado is usually consumed as a dessert, whipped with milk and sugar.

• blue cheese - most Burmese know only cheddar cheese which they think is the same as Kraft, the processed cheese spread.

• rare beef - a frightening sight to most Burmese, women especially.

Large quantities of about four dishes, followed by fruit and/or dessert (a kind that is stretchable like custards or cakes) should be enough to cover a whole evening. This is usually the custom at feasts when the Burmese entertain.

You may find that your guests do not eat much and this can well be because they have already eaten *before* coming to your party! This is because dinner time for most Burmese is around 5.30 or 6.30 p.m. (all meal times are generally earlier because the day starts at about 5.30 a.m.) Thus, if invitations are for around 7.30 p.m. or even later, it is unavoidable that your guests will have eaten something before coming over. This also saves them losing face by appearing exceedingly hungry!

Your guests may also leave rather early. As mentioned earlier, making small-talk and dinner party conversation is rather hard for them. Their bedtimes are also very early compared to Western standards.

Men and women will often segregate at buffets and other gatherings. Women tend to huddle together, being rather modest and shy. This is culturally ingrained and no woman would risk getting herself branded a "bold hussy" by going over to the men's groups and joining a discussion. Neither is it because they are uninformed. In many gatherings the wives of officials are school teachers or hold high positions in government offices. They can also probably speak English and most will have a university degree. It's just that it isn't the done thing and it's unlikely this behaviour will change just yet.

Buffets and Cocktails

These two types of entertainment are worth mentioning because most Burmese seem to find them boring and uncomfortable. Burmese find it hard to eat while standing up and, even worse, standing to eat *and* drink.

When Burmese have a large crowd to a meal the group takes turns to eat at the table starting from the eldest and the youngest (children and babies), with the womenfolk coming last. Guests are never subjected to having to balance plates, cutlery and drinks while standing or having to sit on sofas. A comfortable position is important in enjoying a meal for the Burmese.

Finger foods and snacks are not defined as a proper meal and again Burmese tend to eat their dinner at home before going to cocktails and receptions. At the reception they will just nibble.

Buffets and cocktails are also uncomfortable for them because of the need for small talk. If spouses are invited they particularly tend to be tongue-tied because they simply do not know how to handle conversation with strangers or unfamiliar people. Most Burmese are intimidated by Caucasians, expecting a vast difference in cultural norms and in points of interest.

In addition, alcohol is not usually consumed so that cocktail parties may end up with most of the guests only accepting soft drinks!

Question Time

At dinners or other social occasions you will almost certainly be asked by Burmese whether you have sampled their local foods yet and which ones you liked. Burmese love to hear that you like *mohinga* (if

143

you really do). Food and cakes may be sent over to you if you are neighbours.

You will be asked how you like other things in Burma. You will impress people if you go prepared with a little knowledge about Burmese clothes and fabrics, especially handwoven textiles.

Be sure to respond positively to questions about Burmese beaches and towns such as Mandalay and Pagan. Talk about the fresh air and the exotic Burmese fruits and flowers rather than the lack of entertainment or the irregular electricity and water supply. The people in Burma have learnt to live without night entertainment for years. They talk, sleep early, turn to religion and watch videos when they can. This is probably a healthy lifestyle, except for the high cost and generally low quality of nutritious food.

The point is, be positive about things Burmese. Never compare the place or its features negatively with your own home country – at least not in conversation.

Words of Invitation When Eating

Htine ba	Please sit down.
Saar ba	Please eat.
Aar ya paar ya saar ba	Please eat heartily
Saar ba, ah ma na ba nai	Please do eat, do not feel *ah-nar-de*.

— Chapter Six —

TRAVELLING INSIDE BURMA

If you are living in Burma for some time, there will be occasions when you travel. Burma is a large country and there are a variety of scenic places to visit. However, many areas are out of bounds to foreigners and even the Burmese themselves have never been to the further reaches and mountainous areas of their country due to the difficulty of travelling. The poor communications infrastructure means that travel is exhausting and uncomfortable, as well as time-consuming.

Some parts of the country are also quite dangerous to visit as there are wild animals, armed rebels from the ethnic minorities and robbers (known as *dacoits*). However, things are slowly changing for visitors.

Foreigners are now allowed to travel as far north as Lashio and this may be extended in the near future, following reports of plans to develop the area around Myitkyina.

WHY DO BURMESE TRAVEL?

For the most part, Burmese travel to the more accessible places in the country to make pilgrimages to famous pagodas. They seldom travel for the sake of taking a relaxing holiday by the sea or in the countryside, as those in developed countries would. Most of their travelling is done during the dry or cool seasons which are off-peak for the agricultural year. It is also the time when the pagodas have their annual festivals known as *hpaya-pwe*.

The rest of the time, the travellers one would be likely to meet on trains or buses are usually either students going back home during holidays or merchants on business trips.

As times are hard now for the common people, they are unable to travel much unless an emergency, such as the death or illness of a family member, requires personal attendance.

Tickets for air journeys are very hard to obtain. As for most goods, there is a black market in tickets and the price is many times that of the real fare. If they can be afforded, one then has to suffer the departure and arrival delays common in Burma. The situation is the same for rail travel and it is easier to travel by car or bus. Water transport is unsafe and nearly always uncomfortable.

Places of historical interest or beauty do not seem to draw the Burmese as much as significant Buddhist attractions such relics or monks reputed to have mystical powers. They seldom go sightseeing for its own sake, religious concerns seeming to be more important to them. Anyway, economic circumstances demand that travel has to be more than just for fun. One might as well aim to gain religious merit at the same time!

Thus, a wonder like Pagan, with its ancient architecture, paintings, murals and sculptures, has been more acclaimed by Westerners than

The terrace of the Shwe Dagon is always full of devotees perambulating clockwise or anticlockwise.

Burmese. For most Burmese such beauty has little worth in its own right without religious significance.

PLACES TO SEE

The well-travelled circuit for foreign visitors is Mandalay, Maymyo, Pagan, Taunggyi, Sandoway and Pegu. These places are often described in the tourist and back-packer's guidebooks.

Less visited towns are Moulmein, Pyinmana, Toungoo, Bassein, and Prome, all of which are typical Burmese towns but not as full of cultural interest as those mentioned above. However, it may be that you will visit these places for business purposes as they are centres with traditional crafts and marketable products.

Burma is a land of pagodas and within the towns they will be the most obvious sights. Many of them are centuries old. In Rangoon, the Shwe Dagon on Singuttara Hill is the most sacred pagoda in Burma

147

as it enshrines Buddha's hair and other sacred relics. Gold and precious gems adorn the pagoda and are buried in the main treasure chamber under the spire. The main platform and surrounding terraces provide many interesting nooks and crannies and they are always full of worshippers making offerings, meditating and telling beads.

Also in Rangoon, the National Museum, the smaller shrines and the many public monuments provide great photographic material. Other places of interest include the Zoological Gardens, the Aquarium, the Aung San Market, The Martyrs Mausoleum and the two lakes, Inya and Royal Lake.

However, many consider Mandalay the true capital of Burma and feel that its atmosphere is also more Burmese than Rangoon's. Mandalay Hill provides a spectacular view of the city, its many pagodas and famous monasteries. The palace here has also been restored.

From Mandalay you can go to Ava, Sagaing or Amarapura, all of which were once capitals in Burma's history. Alternatively you could visit the cool hills of colonial Maymyo.

In Pegu, about 45 miles north of Rangoon, there are some of the oldest ruins in Burma, as well as more pagodas. On the road to Pegu you will have a chance to see the paddy fields and typical Burmese villages. The War Cemetery is also on this road.

Pagan is usually on most visitor's lists. If you are going to see the beautiful art and architecture of the pagodas, be prepared for walks and climbs - you can climb some pagodas right to the top terraces.

Taunggyi, Kalaw and Inlay Lake are usually combined in one visit, with a tour of the Pindaya caves thrown in. In summer these places are refreshingly cool but temperatures can reach freezing point in December and January. Inlay Lake is famous for its boatsmen who row with their legs.

Sandoway beach in the Arakan state and the newly developed Chaung Tha beach near Bassein are both clean and have modern facilities. Some of the wealthy Burmese from Rangoon and Mandalay have beach holidays here, but such holiday-makers are the exception to the rule in Burma. The Tavoy area also has long stretches of beach but these remain undeveloped, the beach bungalows inhabited only by locals.

THINGS TO BUY

Shopping for products not available in one's home town is of course an added bonus for Burmese travellers.

When travelling in the Shan states it is mainly fruits that are brought home. Those that can't be carried at least can be eaten up on the way! Favourite fruits to buy here are strawberries, avocados, oranges and tangerines. A visit to a traditional Five Day Market in the Shan region is a particularly colourful sight as the local ethnic people, wearing their ethnic dress, will come to sell their wares. You may also discover some interesting woven textiles, woollen shawls and thick *longyi* at such markets because of the colder climate here.

Mandalay offers a variety of good buys, especially from the Zegyo Market. These include leather goods like slippers and bags; woven fabrics made into *longyi* and shoulder bag;, tapestries (called *kala gar*); pieces of bark for grinding into *thanaka*; and a whole variety of speciality foods. Gold leaf is also made in Mandalay. This is applied to Buddha images by devotees during worship.

Pagan is the place to buy quality lacquerware, while Prome is famed for its custard apples and textiles similar to *ikat*. The Arakan state offers seafood and thicker *longyi* that come in regional chain designs. Fruit preserves, coconut wafers and *jaggery* are specialities of the Tenasserim strip.

WHERE TO STAY

Burmese travellers usually stay with relatives, who are always expected to offer their hospitality, even if it's only in the form of a space to put one's bedroll. Monasteries are also open to overnight guests if the chief abbot or monk is requested. However, women can only stay in monasteries if they have accompanying menfolk and then only in designated buildings. Foreign guests may also be allowed to stay in the monasteries but should be careful to dress and behave appropriately. On leaving, a moderate donation should be offered.

Government civil servants on tour duty usually stay at circuit houses, used since colonial times. Most of these circuit houses have a history of being haunted by ghosts. In fact, in one case, the ghost was asked to guard the house and is said to continue to do so!

Foreign guests can be sure to get good accommodation since Burmese hosts will go out of their way to make everything as pleasant as possible for them. Similarly, for high-ranking government officials, guest houses suddenly have soap, towels and toilet paper, all of which were missing before. The wish to please is so great that the honoured guest will be offered articles that the hosts themselves cannot afford for daily use.

Hotels are available in the main sightseeing towns like Mandalay, Pagan and Taunggyi. By law, local people are forbidden to accommodate foreign visitors in their houses. Possibly this rule may be relaxed in the future, especially as tourism is being recognised as a means of earning precious foreign exchange. Even now many small, privately-owned guest houses and inns are springing up in the larger cities.

PRE-TRAVEL PREPARATION

Before you travel, try to find out as much as possible about your destination, journey, the towns through which you will be travelling and the climate of the region. If you have hosts, it will also help to find out about them too, so that you can be sure of forms of address, what to expect, how to behave and so on.

Burmese Travel Necessities

At the station, jetty or even the airport, you will see the local traveller's luggage. This usually includes his bedding: a light *kapok* mattress, a woven mat, a pillow, a light cotton blanket and mosquito net, all rolled up neatly and tied with a strong plastic rope.

Other luggage will include beverages in flasks or bottles, food in a carrier, various gifts for the hosts in return for his bed and meals, and a few clothes in an overnight bag.

Your Travel Kit

Whether you are entering Burma on a short visit or travelling within the country while living there, you should take with you the following things:

- Medicine such as aspirin, diarrhoea pills, calamine lotion, antihistamines if you are prone to allergies, malaria tablets and one course of antibiotics. Other drugs and injections such as insulin and disposable needles for diabetics, and relevant emergency medication for asthmatics.
- Cotton wool and bandaids.
- Water purifying tablets.
- Cosmetics.
- Personal needs such as shampoo, toothpaste, soap and some soap powder or detergent for a small amount of laundry.
- Tissues, Wet Ones, your own toilet rolls.
- Can-opener.
- Torch.
- Candles, lighter or matches.
- Swiss army knife.
- Clothing, including disposable underwear, sanitary towels or pads, socks (extra pairs if you cannot go around barefoot), warm clothes like sweaters, cardigans (see also *Clothing* below).
- Insect repellents like ointments, sprays and mosquito coils or insect killers.

Clothing

Clothing depends on which area you will be visiting. Rangoon has a moderate climate and during the day it is warm. The coldest period is in December and January at night-times.

Long flared skirts and trousers are good for sightseeing, especially as sights are bound to include several pagodas where you may have to sit on mats to rest. For ladies, shorts and miniskirts are not advisable, nor is going around without a bra. Burmese are modest and find this type of dressing offensive and shocking. A certain immorality is attached to one who dresses this way, the logic being that if you are not ashamed of exposing yourself you are capable of doing other things! Upper arms are also better covered, not just for modesty's sake but to avoid sunburn and insect bites.

Warm clothing is needed for hill areas like Maymyo, even though this place is close to Mandalay, which is one of the hottest regions in Burma. Taunggyi and Kalaw, which are on the Shan Plateau, are also popular hill resorts and require sweaters and woollens. Remember that in such places the locals use hot bricks to warm their beds and boil water if they want hot baths.

Mandalay is always warm but has soaring temperatures during summer. If you are visiting there you would need light clothing only. However, because Mandalay is close to Maymyo, which you may also decide to visit, you should take along some warmer clothes too.

The Big "Shoe Question"

Shoes will have to be removed every time you enter a temple so it is best to wear ones that are without laces or can be easily removed and put on again. Sandals will be comfortable and practical, but trainers or hiking boots with a lot of laces may not be so convenient when sightseeing in the towns. They are more suitable for a long journey and for walking in areas like Pagan, where one must climb hills and walk amongst thorny scrub.

The big "shoe" question concerning the need to remove shoes is a difficult and sensitive subject. In the past, it was even considered a sufficient reason to start a war: King Narathihapate executed the Mongol diplomatic mission when they did not remove their shoes for a royal audience! Similarly, a British missionary craving a royal audience with King Bodawpaya was refused when he entered the royal palace wearing his shoes.

The custom of having to remove shoes is one that does irk, not just for the discomfort but for the doubtful cleanliness of most surfaces. Local signs saying "Footwearing Prohibited" may bring smiles to most visitors' faces but they should also be obeyed.

In the neighbouring country of Thailand, shoes can be worn on the terraces of pagodas and must be removed only inside the pavilions and shrines. In Burma, however, one has to leave footwear at the very entrance to pagoda and monastery grounds. You therefore have to climb the stairs and walk around the pagoda terraces barefoot.

In the case of a very large pagoda, such as the Shwe Dagon, the terraces are kept clean by voluntary cleaning associations, but you may still tread on pigeon droppings, puddles and miscellaneous litter. The safest thing is to wear socks. Failing that, be sure to wash your feet as soon as you get back to your hotel or home.

BEHAVIOUR AT RELIGIOUS SITES

In places like Pagan, you will find relics and antiques lying around all over the place, that is if they have not already been destroyed by vandalism or stolen by locals and other visitors.

It is better not to yield to temptation and pick up something for a souvenir. You may be tempted by thoughts like: "If I don't take it, someone else will", "If I leave it, it will only be vandalised" or "At least it will be taken good care of in my collection." There is no adequate protection of these valuable antiques and the local sense of heritage is not so great as the need to get some money for the next meal.

On the other hand, being taken on a round of all the pagodas may well daze you so much that you are not be able to appreciate the treasures or the architectural splendour. Some sites are not very well-preserved and museum pieces may seem insignificant because a lack of know-how means they are poorly displayed. However, do try to be positive and express admiration rather than complaint. Remember that Burma has been closed for so long people have had to survive by various means, including the destruction of their own art treasures.

Moreover, some objects and handicrafts on sale do not have high degrees of refinement as materials may have been poor to start with. Sometimes fakes purporting to be from Burma, but actually made in neighbouring countries, seem ever so much better!

When you are in the pagodas or monasteries remember that women should not attempt to talk or shake hands with monks as they are forbidden to touch the female sex. Monks may even turn their backs to women when they pass.

Donating money to them does not mean that you simply hand over the cash. It should be placed in an envelope and then handed to the monks' attendant (*kappiya*).

Religious objects inside shrines may be photographed and there are rarely restrictions on photography.

Too much laughter and loud talk is probably best avoided, although there is no strict rule about this.

The pagodas of Pagan are some of the most beautiful sights in Burma.

GIFTS FOR YOUR HOSTS

When you travel in Burma and want to choose gifts for friends you visit or your host, it is always best to note which products are scarce in their area. The Burmese themselves go by this rule. For example, where the town is located inland, gifts of dried fish, shrimp or other coastal/freshwater products are appreciated. This again applies with fruits, speciality foods, textiles and consumer goods. (See Chapter Five for more on gift-giving).

— Chapter Seven —

SETTLING IN

Foreigners living in Burma are invariably uncomfortable at first. This is often due to a vast difference in standards of living between Burma and the places from which they have arrived. Rangoon seems positively primitive with its uncertain electricity and water supply, lack of supermarkets and consumer products, and no nightlife. One Western friend summarised her annoyance in a memorable line, "There's no ice in the hotel, no nightlife, just lots of pagodas!"

At least those who have previously spent time in Burma are happy to find nothing has changed when they return! Those who are already aware of the conditions are able to get adjusted more quickly. By the time they leave they can appreciate Burma for its positive qualities: the fresh air, unspoiled beaches, green trees - relatively rare qualities these days.

HOUSE FOR RENT

Brokers will help you find a house and put you in touch with potential landlords or landladies. There are large numbers of houses specifically built to be rented out to expatriates for foreign exchange, so there is a good choice available, especially in Rangoon.

Getting the right broker is important. You should preferably contact them through friends so that you can draw from their experience and advice, should you need it. Common problems to look out for include brokers failing to refund when a deal falls through; unreliable brokers who will show you all kinds of unsuitable accommodation in a desperate attempt to make a deal; and disagreements over the brokerage fee (although this is usually fixed at a month's rent).

Suburbs outside Rangoon, towards the north, are good residential areas and have a concentration of accommodation. Houses are really a better choice than apartments as they normally have walls and gates which offer security and privacy. Flats are rather functional in design at present. The typical house for foreigners is either one or two-storeys and has about five or six rooms. The older houses are even bigger. Most houses will have large gardens with shady trees.

Unlike modern cities, where people prefer to stay close to their offices, the demand in Rangoon for such houses has kept residential districts outside the city limits. The centre of Rangoon commands high rents for office space only and residential apartments tend to be old ones with poor water supplies and old fittings.

A building and construction boom appears to have started recently as many modern apartments are being built and planned in Rangoon and the other cities.

Termites and Other Pests

Termites, which Asians also call white ants, can reduce the contents of a cupboard to debris in a day or two. Termites tend to live in areas with reddish soil. They like dark, moist areas and the rains tend to bring more termites into the house.

Oddly, the Burmese take it as a good omen if a white-ant mound appears overnight in their houses and shops (many of which have only earthen floors). The mound may even have gold leaf stuck on it as an offering, the way Buddha images are normally ornamented during worship.

Other common fauna that live in the house are lizards, spiders, geckos, ants (all sizes and colours) and cockroaches. Chemicals can be used but domestic staff should not be allowed to handle pesticides without supervision unless one can be sure they know the dangers of using them. Other pests include rats, mice and occasionally snakes if there is a large garden outside.

As a rule, young children should not be allowed to play in dark, cool corners of the house.

Flooding

Flooding occurs in some parts of Rangoon during very heavy rains. This seems to be due to houses being built along areas which form natural drains for rainwater.

Flooding causes great damage to lovely teak parquet floors and, of course, to furniture and carpets. These should be moved upstairs, if you have an upstairs. Most houses are raised anyway, but if you are thinking of looking for a house on a hill to avoid flooding, think again - you may find that the water supply doesn't reach the second floor! Arranging for a pump to be installed can be troublesome and costly.

Power Supply

Three-phase wiring is recommended as your electrical load is expected to be heavy by Burmese standards. Electricity is a 220 voltage system but is irregular and, as this can do irreparable damage to fridges, computers and other appliances, it is worthwhile having a power regulator installed.

In fact, in Burma appliances are better investments if they are manual rather than electric, not only because of the unpredictable power supply but because of domestics, who may be unskilled with such tools. In any case, you should get into the habit of never leaving electrical appliances with unsupervised servants. They may be honest and intelligent but they are sometimes illiterate or may have no idea of the danger of appliances. Unless you are sure of their capabilities, ban them from using electrical equipment, then at least you have only yourself to blame if expensive tools get broken or accidents happen.

You need to keep rechargeable electric lights, candles and matches for use during black-outs. These tend to be frequent and occur without warning. Stand-up fans may be needed as an alternative to air-cons. However, most houses will have ceiling fans and large verandahs that can help to keep rooms cool.

DOMESTICS

How many staff do you need? The average well-to-do Burmese household has at least one maid and up to three in large houses or families. These maids will do the cleaning, laundry (all washing is done manually) and cooking, as well as looking after any young children. A driver and very probably his family may live in the servants quarters as it is common for whole families to be hired in some domestic capacity by a wealthy household.

Nowadays full-time gardeners are seldom kept by those with big gardens because part-time workers are quite willing to come for a day to trim the grass and the hedges.

As you are likely to be living in a big house, you may at least need someone to do the cleaning. However, many expatriates in Asia find domestic help cheap and convenient, so maids will often live-in and act as a cook and nanny as well. You will soon get used to such a lifestyle when you begin to find yourself occupied with sightseeing trips, travelling, entertaining and other expatriate activities.

Butlers are not really necessary any more and drivers can sometimes double as butlers on occasions when you are entertaining.

Finding Good Staff for Your Household

There are networks of brokers who will bring lots of prospective maids for you to consider or try out. These brokers make a considerable amount of money by going from one household to another and moving these girls about, earning brokerage each time. A common tale when they wish to remove a maid from your household is that one of her relatives, either father, mother or grandmother, has been taken ill and is about to die. Can she go back to the village as soon as possible?

Sometimes the story may be true and you should remember the importance of visiting the sick and attending funerals in Burmese culture. However, sometimes the maids themselves are also looking for another job that will be more congenial and they are so simple that they believe the next household is sure to be better. The brokers will also fuel this belief since the more times a maid is employed the more brokerage he earns.

Diplomatic corps and UN personnel tend to acquire staff from those who are leaving, a sort of hand-me-down system which seems to work quite well. However, be aware that every household does things differently and what was good for previous employers may not be good enough for you. It should be made clear from the beginning the way you wish things to be done.

The majority of domestic staff are Karens or Indians who can speak English because of Christian education. They also tend to be knowledgeable of Western practices, habits and methods of cooking and housekeeping. Other missionary-educated ethnic groups are also Christians. However, one expatriate lady who responded to a questionnaire for this book did mention a situation in which her Karen maid pointedly refused to serve a guest of Indian origin. Problems with habits and customs will arise even with domestics who appear more Westernised than others.

The Burmese themselves do not tend to work as domestics because they generally find it beneath them to be employed in such jobs. Nevertheless, remuneration in foreign exchange can be an important factor in recruitment. Jobs as drivers and chauffeurs also appear to be more in line with their concept of status and prestige, and there seem to be many young Burmese male graduates who seem quite happy with such employment.

Sometimes very young "green" girls are passed off as experienced staff because of the higher wage and resulting brokerage that can be earned. If you suspect that a young girl cannot possibly have as much experience in cooking and cleaning as your broker claims, you might bargain for a lower price or insist on a trial period.

In some cases young girls can be trained easily, especially if they have some education. They can become very faithful and attached to their employers and the children they look after. Indeed, you will find that for most of the locals, a job is rarely a job in its objective sense. It has all the ramifications of a social relationship. Some employers have been known to take a particular member of their staff back home with them when they left, they had become so much a part of the family.

In choosing staff, personal cleanliness and orderliness as well as a good character should be essentials.

Control

Domestic staff, however reliable, will still need a clear definition of what is expected of them. Rules must be established and control exerted. If you don't, you may find that, especially with household expenses, you are being presented with large inflated bills. It is advisable to make yourself knowledgeable about prices, weights and measures (see page 169-70) in order to have a rough idea of whether or not you are being over-charged. Always ask local friends, who will be only too happy to help you with such information.

However, too much control is difficult as is too little. You don't want to be patronising and insulting as this creates a bad atmosphere in your house. You will have to measure the trustworthiness of each member of your staff on an individual basis.

In many cases it is wise to overlook small or trivial shortcomings if you find that overall performance is adequate. Because of the language barrier alone, there will be many things which cannot be explained to you. Standards differ from place to place and Burma is one of those countries where most of the population do not have anything to do with foreigners, let alone attempt to understand their customs and ways. Adequate performance is more feasible than nagging your domestics to do things exactly as you would do them and have them walk out on you.

Once you have trained them it becomes a frightening prospect to think of doing the same again for a succession of servants. If the latter does occur, you should be warned that there is no such thing as the perfect domestic.

When Things Aren't Right

Scolding your staff is a sensitive issue. Always be sure to give a proper explanation when you want things to be done in a particular way. Keep your anger controlled and, above all, do not shout. Be sure that the staff understand that you are criticising the way things are done and not the person himself/herself. Shame is hard to bear in Burmese culture, so never do your scolding in front of other staff. Take the person aside and do it quietly.

Remember that you do depend on them. Although you may have done everything "back home" single-handedly, here in Burma things are different: the house is large, the shopping is different, the cooking is different and there are also a lot of other things you would rather be doing in a new country than all that housework.

In many cases the staff may not understand you properly. You may not have made an instruction very clear and, instead of asking again, they do what they think you meant. Most times they will not have the courage to ask you anything, let alone question your instructions. Moreover, when you scold them they may not be articulate enough to explain how a mistake came about, so you do need to be very patient.

Who's the Boss?

Egalitarian approaches to domestic management do not work. Although you may very much want to treat domestics as equals, you will be unable to do so or find it working against you.

The master and the mistress of the house are usually perceived as being at the highest level, and you cannot change that. They will not eat at the same table or sit on the same sofa. But, in a way, this makes things easy when it comes to difficult situations where you have to explain something that you are not happy with and exert your authority. Giving too much freedom and then taking it away will leave your staff wondering where they stand. Be kind and understanding, but clear and firm. You will be appreciated for it.

Even if you do not attempt to control much, it is a good idea to at least be visible. For example, get up early (you can always disappear again later) and give some instructions about what is to be cooked or your family's programme for the day. This gives broad guidelines to your domestics and it shows that you are the boss around the house.

Privacy

In your new home the setting may be very grand and who would complain about the luxury of being waited on hand and foot? Nevertheless, when you have domestics it becomes very difficult to have privacy.

One solution is to give the servants a day off while you enjoy the company of your husband/wife and children. Alternatively you could all take off somewhere where there will be no servants. Each of these measures safeguards against tempers becoming frayed because of constant domestic companionship.

Security

Valuables should be kept under lock and key or watched constantly. Stolen things are rarely recovered and you should remember that even everyday things are of value in Burma. It is sometimes a good policy to give away what you can before someone else does it for you. In other words, such things as outgrown or never-worn clothes, old and forgotten toys, books and stationery should be passed on to someone who will appreciate them. Even empty cans, containers and bottles can be sold. Possibly the person who is highest in the pecking order among your domestics (usually the longest-serving member) can be allowed to supervise a fair distribution of these.

A Word About Pets and Other Animals

Burmese do not generally keep pets, but if they do it is mostly cats or dogs. Rather than pedigree dogs, which are not hardy and are expensive to feed and take care of, *pariah* dogs (mongrels) are more commonly kept as guard dogs. Some families may keep fish, rabbits, guinea pigs and birds but because of economic hardship it is not common to keep pets.

Nevertheless, the Burmese try to be kind to animals because of their Buddhist ethic. You will find people feeding stray dogs and cats but they will not take them home. Large snails which wreak havoc in gardens will just be collected and dumped somewhere else, only to come back and start eating the leaves all over again. Similarly, rats and mice will not be poisoned but trapped and thrown out. At one time there was a superstition that rats would move away if one wrote on the kitchen wall, "Rats for Sale". Presumably the rodents had to be literate for the trick to work! Live fish found among those bought from the market during shopping will be released if possible.

These actions are the result of the Buddhist belief that animals

165

Buddhists like to release birds from captivity to gain merit.

must not be harmed and that merit is obtained by releasing animals from captivity. However, for the ceremony of releasing, someone has first to incur the evil of catching the animals! It is generally believed to be evil to keep living creatures in captivity.

The point is that if you have brought pets with you, you should make sure you have staff who will be able to take care of them. While the Burmese generally treat animals kindly, they are not used to pampering them as pets. Some domestics will be offended at being asked to clear up after dogs and cats. This may not make for the most hygienic environment either, as your staff may also be handling food as well as cleaning.

Local dogs and cats are nearly always stray ones and therefore likely to be carriers of worms, fleas and ticks. It may be easy for your own pets to catch these infestations, not to mention your children.

It is a good idea to keep watch dogs in the garden at night. They should be kept away from the fence and the gate so that poisoned food cannot be fed to them by potential thieves. Female pets should be sterilised to prevent litters from strays, which you will find wandering all over the place. Local vets can carry out surgical spaying although you may need a local friend or contact to avail yourself of these services.

SHOPPING

Going to the market with one of your domestics can be an educational experience, but you may be daunted by the prospect of dealing with stall owners who don't speak English and are always on the lookout to rip-off unwary customers. Even Burmese customers can be "had" if they do not watch out, especially since some of them are reluctant to bargain and do not enjoy it at all.

Some of the markets, locally known as bazaars, are very wet and dirty. When you go there it is better to wear wooden clogs which are high and help to keep your feet clean. You could buy a pair and keep them in the car.

You need a basket or two with you as plastic bags are still not widely available. Leaves and twine are still used to wrap meat and vegetables.

Most of the food tends to be watery. For example, prawns and shrimp are mixed with ice which later melts, and fresh fish drips blood when chopped into pieces. Adulteration with water is also common as it increases weight. So, if you're not careful you can end up with a smelly car or boot after a trip to the market. A practical measure is to keep a large metal tray in the car boot to put your shopping bags or baskets on.

As a foreigner, you will be very conspicuous in the local market, especially if you are Caucasian. Even if you are Asian, the fact that you are wearing a dress or trousers will make you distinct. For that reason alone you are easy prey. Thus, it is better to shop with friends or with staff for some time, until you can achieve a rapport with certain shop and stall owners who you can regularly patronise. In Burmese you will become known as *hpao thei* (a favourite customer). This will make shopping easier and undoubtedly save time with bargaining. Your stall owners will also get to know you by sight which is important as, to Asians, Caucasians all look the same (and probably vice versa). Most stall owners can speak enough English to conduct business.

However, because of the lack of availability and dubious quality of goods in the markets, many foreigners get supplies from abroad. Foods like biscuits, cheese, mayonnaise, butter and drinks are either stocked up on trips abroad or may be bought at the US Embassy. Japanese expatriates are also said to fly in plane-loads of food items.

Money

Kyat are counted in thousands and tens of thousands. K100 000 is called a *lakh* (derived from the Indian system) or a *theinn* in Burmese. One million *kyat* is called a *crore* (Indian) or *gaday* (Burmese).

Any statistical tables concerning money will use these terms.

MEASURES
Burmese counting and measuring is a system of its own and must be
learned by anyone who wishes to shop successfully.

Weight
Weight is measured in viss (*peik-tha*) and ticals (*kyat thar*). A viss is
about 3.3 lbs (1.5 kg) There are 100 ticals in a viss. So, a tical is
roughly half an ounce (14 g)

All shops in the bazaar selling provisions by weight would use this
measure. However, rice is weighed differently, the basic measure
being the condensed milk can (*bu*). Eight of these make up a *pyi*
(usually measured in a small basket). Sixteen of these baskets make
a *tinn* (usually put in a gunny or jute bag).

Length
Length is still measured in *gaik* (pronounced gike).

One *gaik* is one yard (91 cm).

One *taung* is $^1/_2$ a yard (45.5 cm).

One *htwa* is a $^1/_4$ of a yard (22.75 cm).

One *might* is one $^1/_8$ of a yard (11.37 cm).

Food Measures
- Fruits are measured by units. Ask for the price per apple, per
  pomelo, per mango and so on. Alternatively ask for the price of 5
  or 10 pieces.
- Dried raisins and other dried fruits are measured by weight. Ask for
  the price per viss or for 50 ticals.
- Small fruits, such as local sour plums, are bought by the condensed
  milk can. Ask for the price per *tinn* or *pyi*.
- Fresh coffee and tea are by the pound (0.45 kg).
- Meat, fish and shrimps are in quantities of 10 ticals.
- Flowers are by the stalk, garland or bunch (*d'see*).
- Biscuits are by the pound or viss.

- Milk is by the viss.
- Oil is by the viss or 100 viss.
- Potatoes are by the viss.
- Leafy vegetables are by the bunch.
- Large vegetables, such as marrow and aubergines (eggplant), are per piece or, sometimes, even by the number of slices.
- Eggs are by number.
- Soya sauce is by the bottle.
- Fish sauce is by the viss.

Textiles

- Textiles are generally by the yard.
- Woven sarong fabric is by the piece. On average, this is 2 yards (1.82 m) of a standard 1 yard (91 cm) width.

Others

- Medicine may be sold per tablet or capsule, as well as by the bottle.
- Petrol/gasoline is by the gallon (pronounced "ga-lan").

These are general guidelines only to show how quotations vary from item to item. You can see the great variety of units used. Note that the Keighley Wholesale Market beside the river in Rangoon (now known as the People's Market) has seasonal vegetables and fruit at wholesale prices.

Bargaining

Government-owned shops will have fixed prices, but elsewhere bargaining extensively is needed only where prices are obviously high. In most cases where prices are only a little above what you know to be the average, it may not be worth the hassle of bargaining on a daily basis.

However, in the case of clothes or fabric, the price quoted might be double or more the true price. You will have to find fault with the goods in question in order to give the seller the chance of lowering his price without a great loss of face.

Throughout this process you must not show anger or impatience. If you do, you are already the loser. Burmese customers often walk away from a stall so that the seller will call them back and give them a better price, although sometimes he may even call their bluff and let them leave. However, be reasonable. He is in business and has to make a profit, not just break even.

Keep your cool and be persistent but charming. Be good-humoured and give in with grace if you want to buy an item badly enough but are unable to get a lower price. Alternatively, get your local friends to buy it for you if you must have it. The only trouble with this is that they may decide to give it to you as a present and you could find yourself insisting on repaying them the money. If this is the case, all you can do is give them some other present in return.

Never bargain for an item and then leave the shop without buying it. This is very bad bargaining manners and suggests you lack finesse. It is best to make sure that an item is something you really want before you start to bargain for a lower price. Otherwise you'll be obliged to take something which you were only vaguely interested in.

HEALTH AND EMERGENCIES
The tropical weather and the unusual food can easily cause health problems for visitors.

The extreme heat in the daytime also makes one perspire, which tends to cause colds and flu. Coughs are usually thick and, because of the climate, take some time to go away. For such minor ailments, your own medicine chest should be sufficient.

In other cases, the best medicine is preventive medicine. Remember that tap water is unsafe for drinking and must always be boiled. When you eat out, keep away from uncooked food, ice in drinks, raw vegetables and cut fruit. Fruit should be washed in your own home and then cut before eating.

Don't rush to experience everything local all at once. Slow exposure may build up some immunity, but even then one should be careful.

In the absence of food and drug laws, antibiotics and other products that would normally be dispensed only on prescription can be freely purchased in the local market. However, you should really be careful when buying drugs like this. It is best to bring in your own supplies if you can, bearing in mind the expiry date on medicine packets and bottles.

During your stay you may take trips to the more developed countries near Burma. When you do, it is a good idea to plan some time to seek medical treatment for less urgent problems and to stock up on medicines that are in low supply.

For serious ailments that cannot wait, there are clinics with good reputations. The Diplomatic Hospital has specialist doctors who attend to expatriates, visitors and the diplomatic corps.

The University Hospital is small but could attend to emergencies. There is also the Yangon General Hospital, other private clinics and hospitals.

Burmese contacts are necessary in order to get quick action.

EDUCATIONAL FACILITIES

Before the nationalisation of all schools there were many private institutions, mostly set up by the missions before the Second World War. Children of foreigners often attended these schools as classes were in English. The University also held classes in English.

However, since the 1960s all education has been conducted in Burmese, except of course for English classes. Foreign children are thus unable to join local schools but must be sent to the International School. Alternatively, they can go to boarding school back home or in neighbouring countries like Singapore, Thailand and India.

There is a Japanese school in Burma to cater for the large number of Japanese expatriates.

RECREATION

Many visitors to Burma complain of the lack of a "proper" nightlife, even in the capital and major cities. Nightclubs, discos, massage parlours do not exist...yet. Karaoke lounges are just becoming popular in Rangoon.

Local Burmese spend small fortunes on video recorders and spend their free time watching the latest movies (foreign and local), sports events and popular songs and shows in the comfort of their own homes. Video tapes from abroad are all copied as Burma has no copyright laws at present.

Cinemas mostly show the very popular Hongkong *kung fu* movies and cheaper Western movies, such as Italian cowboy films. Local movies are usually heavy drama of the soap-opera kind, dealing with family life, moral dilemmas, youth and student problems.

Burmese movies resemble Indian movies in many ways: there are a lot of songs and dances, a bit of humour and a bit of pathos. Mothers gasp and die in the arms of long-lost or prodigal children (or vice versa); feasts are always eaten and coy expressions are exchanged between leading actors and actresses. These are accepted cinematic conventions and are acted in stereotypical ways – Burmese actors and actresses have no wish to appear natural!

Lately, video plays in Burmese have become very popular and many young TV stars have risen to fame.

Libraries and Bookshops

Government and educational institutions have their own libraries but these are only open to staff and students. Generally, lack of funds has limited the number of books purchased and imports of books, even textbooks, have been seriously affected by the lack of foreign exchange allocations. In any case, those who can read heavy technical textbooks have dwindled in number.

Libraries at the United States and British embassies have large memberships as those who can read English tend to go there to read

173

newspapers and magazines, as well as books.

Bookshops stock secondhand bestselling novels which can either be loaned on a deposit or bought. Non-fiction and technical books or magazines (some of them stolen from postal channels) end up in such stores. A large number of books are sold off by families as scrap and even valuable books will be among those recycled and made into paper bags and exercise books.

Organised Recreation

Recreation for expatriates include local tennis clubs, golf clubs, sailing clubs, as well as embassy-run softball, tennis and swimming leagues. The Australian Embassy, for example, has a large sports complex and a club house.

TRANSPORTATION

Expatriates in Burma often have their own car and even a chauffeur. If you do your own driving (especially if you're a woman), be careful

The horse-drawn cart is still a popular form of transport in many towns.

of being set up by other vehicles or pedestrians who will stage an accident and then try to extort a sum of money from you.

Trishaw drivers tend to do that, but they are rather few these days and are allowed to ply only in some areas.

Traffic jams have not yet arrived in Rangoon and that may explain why traffic rules do not seem to exist. Cars make U-turns where they shouldn't or drive through red lights, while bikes, motorbikes and scooters all want right of way.

However, if you are caught, traffic police are quick to slap fines on motorists, even for minor offences or when it is pedestrians who are at fault. The motorist in Burma is always wrong, so you just can't win.

When you see official cars it is best to draw aside if you can.

Public Transportation

In Rangoon the pre-war buses are always a source of wonder because they are still running after all these years. Gears are wooden sticks and the floors are wooden planks. They crunch loudly and jerk with every change of gear, so you usually have a lurching, bumpy ride. Nevertheless, things would have been much worse if it wasn't for their existence these many years.

Another well-used means of transport is the pick-up truck. This has a roof and benches in the back, but you can have the comfortable seat in the front with the driver if you pay a bit more. These small trucks are imported, mostly by merchant seamen capitalising on their visits home by reselling them. If you ride in the back, be sure to mind your head when you get on and off as the roof is very low.

All forms of public transportation have a driver and a ticket collector known as a *sa peya* (literally from the English, "spare"). One pays for a ticket but may or may not get one; it depends on the ticket-collector's mood. These *sa peya* often hold a handful of notes lengthwise between their fingers and give you your change from this. However, it is better to have exact money with you since he may well

175

forget to give you your change. Their attitude frequently makes you feel too intimidated to ask!

Small or large "Hino" buses also run. They are always packed and you have to ride them with great care, holding on to something all the time. Even pregnant women can be seen precariously standing on the steps, hanging on. At least they can't go very fast. The roads are not conducive to speeding as they have potholes in areas that are not major thoroughfares.

Trishaws - bicycles with a side-car attached - are called *sy-kar* (from "side-car"). Two people can sit in the side car, one facing front and the other facing back. Very stout people are not advised to ride in this type of vehicle.

Rail transportation is unreliable. Although there is a train which circles the city, it does not appear to be well-used. Rail travel has certainly declined in quality since colonial times and there has been no extensive change in the gauge size of the rail tracks since the British laid them. Their narrowness thus makes for a very uncomfortable ride.

Long-distance coaches run from depots in the suburbs. On the whole, travel by road is preferable to travel by rail, water or air. Consequently, every Burmese family aims to have its own car.

LUGYONE *"COURIER" ACTIVITY*

This is one very Burmese activity which is notable and in which you will find yourself participating if you stay long enough in the country. It is more pronounced now because the closed nature of the country means that the influx of goods between Burma and the outside are very much impeded.

The expatriate Burmese, no matter where they may be living, need to consume things Burmese and hence they need to have things brought over from Burma by *lugyone* - literally a person going your way or the way you ask him to go. If you are looking for a person to accompany you to a certain destination in Burma, you can often tag along with a *lugyone*. Alternatively, if you are looking for someone to carry something to a certain person in a distant place, then a *lugyone* is your man (or woman).

On the other hand expatriate Burmese abroad need to send things to relatives and friends back home, so the *lugyone* can help them out, either for free or for a courier fee which will cover some of their expenses.

Some articles might be needed urgently, such as medical supplies, vaccines, letters, books and spare parts for cars and TV's. In addition, luxury food like chocolates, ice-cream, hamburgers, chicken and even doughnuts are carried. I can remember with gratitude a *lugyone* who brought me oral polio vaccine to be given to my daughter. She carried this all the way from Bangkok in a vacuum flask packed with dry ice. The trouble that some *lugyone* go to can hardly be repaid.

Part of the reason for this activity (which is so constant as to be a nuisance) is the inadequate postal system in Burma. Parcels and letters often go mysteriously missing and consequently nothing of value can be sent this way. Another reason is the difficulty of getting things foreign in Burma and things Burmese in places abroad.

The latter concern is not so bad nowadays as many Asians have migrated to the USA, UK and Australia. As a lot of Burmese cooking ingredients are similar to those used by Indians, Chinese, Thai, Vietnamese, Korean and Japanese, cooking Burmese food in a foreign country is not as impossible as it once was. At one time it used to be that even very strong smelling ingredients like fish paste would have to be carried from Burma by a long-suffering *lugyone* who would find on arrival that all the paste had become moist and leaked all over his clothes! Similarly, Indian mango pickles (pickles made in Burma according to an Indian recipe full of oil and spices) would be carried in luggage and subsequently stain everything when the airplane altitude caused the oil to bubble over.

Nowadays things are neater; pickles are made without the oil, which can be added at the destination and fish paste can be found where there are Thais living. Even the national dish *mohinga* can be bought in a deep-frozen form and carried by merchant seamen who have the use of the ship's freezer! So, Burmese no longer need to hanker for supplies from home.

One exception to this rule is that very Burmese food, *lepet*. This recipe of pickled tea, with its ingredients of garlic, beans, peanuts and sesame seeds, is not available outside Burma and must still be carried by somebody prepared to risk a pungent and oily leakage!

As a foreigner and a visitor, it is more than likely that you will be requested to carry something to or from Burma at one time or another, depending on how well your friends know you and how reliable you seem to be. If you are requested it means that you are honoured enough to be the right person to ask!

On your part, you may either refuse or agree to help with these requests, depending on your ability to carry them. If you agree, it means that you show appreciation for your host's/friend's kindness to you; if you refuse you will possibly be noted as a person without a sense of *ah-nar-hmu*!

Chapter Eight

DOING BUSINESS IN BURMA

As with other Asian cultures, human communication in Burma is oblique or indirect. There is an emphasis on who is friendly with whom and how well. When a favour is received it is important for it to be returned when the occasion or a specific request arises. Those on the receiving end are indebted to their benefactors, the more so if it was an important favour.

As an example, let's say one friend has helped another to get his child into an exclusive school by putting in a word with the principal. Later on, that person may ask the favour to be returned, especially as his was a significant one.

In business relationships these customs are extended. Favours received must be returned, however small.

Where a person requires an introduction to another, it is the custom to seek someone who is a mutual friend and can be the intermediary. This intermediary himself will probably will be someone who owes a favour to one of the parties involved.

The first meeting may not be strictly business. It may be more for the purpose of assessing each other's strengths and weaknesses, and generally getting a "feel" for your new acquaintance's personality. At the first meeting anything apart from business may be covered!

Sometimes even astrological calculations are made to discover whether you are the "right" person with whom to have a business partnership.

Burmese business culture is full of networks and it is very important for social relationships to be maintained and kept smooth at all times. Because family relationships are so extended (even the brother of one's sister-in-law would be considered "family", as would the grandson of one's best friend) almost everyone is related by blood or marriage. Thus, Burmese can always find someone with the connections required for their purposes. No actual business deal may come about for quite some time, but the point is that the connection has been made. One has to be flexible and open to opportunity.

Social relationships are frequently placed before business relationships and business success can rest on the bonds of trust derived from social interaction. In Burma it is hard for business relationships to stand alone and you have to make a special effort to be accepted as a person as well as a businessman. The concept of "face" goes hand-in-hand with business relationships. The Burmese do not like to get into situations where refusal will involve a loss of face.

A BRIEF ECONOMIC HISTORY

Burma is just re-emerging on the world business scene after more than 30 years of isolation and attempts at self-sufficiency. During those years, a socialist economy was in existence, complete with planned targets for every product and service, price controls and bureaucratic managerial procedures.

However, back in 1948, when independence from the British was gained, Burma had its share of Indian and Chinese entrepreneurs, as well as a fledgling group of Burmese businessmen. By the 1960s the industrial sector of the economy was a reasonable size and many consumer products of fair quality were being produced.

The nationalisation of businesses and banks after the *coup d'etat* of 1962 slowly ran these enterprises to the ground, mainly due to inexperienced and indifferent managerial staff. So, by the 1970's there was a dire lack of consumer goods of every kind. Attempts were made to change things by introducing some accountability for profit but, by then, the whole system was too entrenched. There were also chaotic and frequent changes in organisations and managerial levels, as well as a negative incentive system where any mistake could result in the loss of jobs. For most employees it was far safer to carry on with unproductive and inefficient routines than do anything that would rock the boat. Initiative was not rewarded and was not part of a manager's requirements.

The pilferage and waste were also appalling. But the general excuse that everyone gave was that they had to survive somehow. "Survival" indeed justified everything from accepting bribes to stealing state property: stationery, spare parts, raw materials, fans and electrical equipment all went missing from government-owned buildings.

In these years, the most lucrative private business became trading in the black market, handling every consumer product that could not be sufficiently produced by the state-owned factories. The black market was never a clandestine market and virtually anyone who had something to sell joined the bandwagon. In fact, the black market allowed the Burmese to survive in the face of an inefficient government distribution system which rationed everything from matchboxes and spools of thread to rice and oil. Most government shops consisted of empty shelves and indifferent sales staff with vacant stares. Some couldn't even be bothered to answer a customer's questions. Consequently, in 1987, in the midst of a "socialist economy", black market turnover was estimated at 1.5 billion US dollars, between a quarter and a half of the country's product (G.D.P.)!

During the years of rationing under the socialist system, the need to survive became the mother of recycling in Burma. The ethic, still in existence today, is that everything can be repaired and used once more. Nobody throws anything away; a broken umbrella can always be mended or a pair of slippers can be resoled or stitched up.

A look at the pre-war cars still being driven around and the types of spare parts which are being produced on local lathe machines should convince anyone of the ingenuity Burmese people have to make the best out of a difficult situation. That's how Burmese have survived for the last three decades on an outdated technological base.

The amount of waste generated by developed countries seems appalling to Burmese, especially when in some societies whole sets of furniture, mattresses, blankets and pillows are thrown away in preparation for the New Year. In Burma you will find that even the well-to-do will still have old-fashioned furniture, simply because it's still of good quality.

Hyperinflation has meant that even wealthy families have had to skimp on the yearly painting of the house, the upkeep of gardens and other luxuries previously afforded, as basic meals take up large portions of the month's budget. For the poor, three meals a day are now likely to be only one, with lots of rice gruel in between.

LEGAL ASPECTS OF BUSINESS

To date, some business laws have been passed but it would seem that these are lagging behind the economic changes that are taking place. Consequently, foreign businessmen may not feel adequately protected by the law.

Since the pro-democracy demonstrations and the coup of 1988, the chief business law passed has been the Investment Law of Myanmar (November 1988). This allowed liberal foreign investments and was coupled with the removal of restrictions on private sector participation in domestic and foreign trade.

Other laws take the form of directives and orders from the government. The main obstacle seems to be the frequent changes in these directives.

BANKING AND FINANCE

An outdated banking system is still in place in Burma. Everything is done manually and is most inefficient in terms of time and money, as well as being truly exasperating for any one who has to deal with banks regularly; even the locals get fed up with the difficulty of withdrawing their own money.

Under the socialist system the objective of the banks was to monitor each person's bank account and plan the total amount. Because it was, and still is, so hard to withdraw money, even from one's own account, the usual practice has been to keep cash at home or, in the case of businesses, to keep it literally in jute sacks lined up along the walls of the house! The demonetisation of currency, reducing cash balances to nothing overnight, have meant that confidence in the currency and banking is very low. This confidence is unlikely to be restored in the face of a banking system which is based on bureaucratic control rather than commercial concerns.

Current inflation means that transactions involving huge amounts of money have to be carried out. Fresh-from-the-bank bundles of money can also be missing a note or two, requiring trusted helpers to count the stacks of currency. At least the printing of larger denominations would alleviate the problem. Denominations such as the K45 and K90 notes make counting extremely difficult, the only rationale behind them being that they are astrologically calculated figures.

The importance of owning foreign exchange cannot be over-emphasised in such a closed economy as Burma's. The rate of

183

exchange has been arbitrarily kept at a level many times higher than the real rate, despite advice from many quarters that the currency should be devalued to bring it closer to its real worth.

However, there may be hope on the banking horizon in the form of the legal reforms which began in 1989. These have allowed the establishment of three private banks and a few branches of foreign chains. Such competition will probably help to increase the efficiency of the state banks.

BURMESE WORKERS AND THE WORK ETHIC

The work ethic of the socialist system was one that emphasised party membership and activities more than anything else. Work would be abandoned for the sake of party meetings, workers' meetings and rallies. The promotions system also gave great weight to membership so that expertise and experience did not count for much.

State-owned organisations are still burdened by a large number of employees who are not as productive as they could be. Inefficiency is encouraged by the practice of not being able to fire workers, unless perhaps for political reasons.

With the reinstatement of private enterprise it is becoming more evident that, where rewards are real and tangible, workers can be motivated to increase productivity. Direct monetary rewards work much better than vague titles like "Worker of the Year".

A foreign employer can expect willingness to learn and to adapt to new things. Loyalty to the company and the idea of keeping company secrets confidential can also be expected, although you may need to make sure this is explicitly understood at all levels.

Working hours are from 9 a.m. to 4.30 p.m. with weekends closed, at least in government offices. Public holidays are listed in Chapter Two, under Festivals.

The Need To Be Businesslike

For the typical Burmese, being businesslike is hard to differentiate from being mercenary. In traditional society, talking about money is regarded as tasteless, especially where favours are concerned. Payment for every single service and item is not understood and because of this Burmese give (and get) a good deal of things for free. For example, doctors in the family would look after relatives and neighbours for free but would have these favours returned in the form of food and gifts. Burmese get a shock to find they have to pay for a drink of water abroad, when plain tea is provided free at most food stalls in Burma. A friend on a brief study period in the West was disgusted to find that a room-mate paid ten cents after making a call from his phone!

In many state-owned factories it is, and was, the custom to give products away to those with whom one wishes to curry favour. Such "donations" eat away at sales and profits, and no private enterprise would do it without adequate justification. Habits like these are pretty much entrenched and it is customary among Burmese to still want many things for free. Attempts at accounting for every office item used brings on complaints, especially about little things like paper clips and pins: "Oh, but they are so small, surely they can be given for free?" To some extent it's almost like a modern monetary economy has not yet fully developed in Burma. Foreign employers will probably need to set down strict rules about "freebies", making clear what can or cannot be taken or given away.

Management and Supervisory Staff

Choosing local supervisory staff for your company has several advantages: they will know more about handling local workers and dealing with cultural differences. Consequently, they can achieve harmony in the work place.

Although many young people are graduates there is a lot of difference between choosing trained and raw graduates. It is possible to mould raw graduates to the company's requirements, while trained graduates have the obvious advantage of experience.

In making promotions, one should be careful to take into consideration the compatibility of local staff and the cultural perceptions of status and rank. For example, an employee who considers himself to be above another in social status, either because of education, birth or age, may be resentful of working under a person whom he considers his inferior. You will need to develop great tact when confronting the Burmese social hierarchy, complete with its perceptions of "face".

All levels of an organisation are important when you are worried about the progress of your projects and plans. Any little aspect of your project which is unclear to those processing it may result in a total halt because of uncertainty on the part of a junior as to how to proceed. He will not dare (or even know) whom to consult. Thus one has to keep tabs on the progress of projects through every stage and for this you need to be on a certain footing with the people concerned, from the lowliest clerks to the highest officials. Ask any successful business-man and he will tell you how important these relationships are.

Qualifications

The education system in Burma has been sadly deteriorating for years now. The general attitude has been for the state to be concerned with preventing student unrest at all costs. Nationalistic objectives have meant that every subject has been taught in the national language and, coupled with severe under-funding, have led to levels of education no longer being comparable to the rest of the world.

The result of this system has meant outdated teaching materials which can never keep up with translations into the national language and thus skeletal knowledge being taught in an easily digestible form.

Graduates of this system have had to upgrade their skills and knowledge at their own expense by enrolling in private tuition courses. These offer training in subjects which are of a practical and vocational nature, such as accountancy, electrical engineering, mechanical training, computer skills, television repair and maintenance, and English language, to name a few. For this reason, the paper qualifications or degree of a prospective employee may show a B.A. in Geography, for instance, but his real skills may lie elsewhere. He may not even have a certificate to prove these skills and the only way to find out about them would be to offer probation periods for such employees.

Young people are especially eager to learn new things, make a reasonable living and to succeed. They are also very flexible. Because of this it may be worthwhile employing young people even if they only have very basic communication skills and educational qualifications.

In the past, employees in state organisations could not be fired once they were in, but the fact that this is not the practice in private enterprise is well-recognised. Young people are perhaps more likely to learn to understand these values than the older generation and, with this new ethic in mind, efficiency and productivity can be achieved.

Many young Burmese abroad find it hard to get a job on the basis of their degrees because the universities in Rangoon are no longer recognised as the reputable institutions that they once used to be. It is frustrating when students have to study for diplomas abroad, even when they hold a bachelor's degrees in the same subject from Burma. For many, the very exposure to the English medium is worth the effort. And to receive a diploma that has international standing is a great achievement.

Blue-Collar Workers

A lot of things which need accuracy may be done inaccurately simply because the people concerned are inclined to easy-going and non-specific habits. For example, in the villages, if you ask for directions you may get answers like, "As far as a stone's throw away," which could be anything from a few yards to a several hundred feet.

You will need to set the work ethic down since most labourers, if they come from agricultural backgrounds, are more used to working and living in tune with nature and the seasons. They will like to take a nap when they are tired or sit around and talk, basically because agricultural life does not generally call for urgency.

However, most Burmese are eager to learn and can do so very quickly, provided instructions and reasons for doing things in a certain way are clearly understood.

Accidents

Many workers are oblivious to danger and hazards in the workplace. The dangers of using and working around machinery need to be adequately impressed upon them, otherwise they will surely fail to protect themselves in any way.

In Burma, mortality rates are very high and life expectancy is quite low due to poor medical facilities and a generally poor quality of life. Consequently, death is perceived as a common part of life that is unavoidable. It's a case of "when your number's up...". Therefore, no great effort is made to champion the workers' safety rights and claims for compensation are seldom followed up. Similarly, doctors are not sued for mistakes that cause death, as the philosophy is that suing will not bring the dead person back.

Language and Communication

Language barriers could be a problem but may be solved by local managerial and supervisory staff acting as intermediaries. However, you would have to train them to your standards first.

Frankness, openness and direct admissions are rare. Mistakes may be covered up when those concerned try to make amends in a panic. You may also find that your apparently clear instructions have not been carried out at all. Confusion over instructions may lead to work just being shelved because Burmese workers do not like to lose face and come and ask you what you meant.

Although English can be understood, proficiency may not be very high so that it is best to use simple English and not idiomatic speech. As in other Asian countries, Caucasian investors may find it more expedient either to start business with a local partner or obtain local managerial staff of required educational standards and let them take care of lower level management.

Asian-Asian relationships are not expected to cause as much difficulty as Western-Asian relationships. As Burma has been a colony for a long time there is still some lingering resistance to the West and Caucasians. This does not apply so much to young people as they may perceive all things Western as superior, having grown up in an entirely closed country.

Working Relationships

In all relationships, no matter how you may try to divide them into social and professional groups, you will find social considerations always have weight. As a superior, you will be looked upon as a father and a teacher if your subordinates really like you.

You may be asked for loans in crises, as well as for shelter or food and advice. You may well have to disappoint them in these requests but try to offer positive alternatives. This will help you prevent loss of face and, consequently, respect.

When making criticisms of work errors, it is a good idea not to do it in front of other staff. Take your subordinate aside and do the scolding quietly in your own office. Avoid shouting and make sure your reasons for the correction are clearly understood so that your employee knows you are criticising work procedures and not him personally. If necessary, formal training should be given in order to orient employees to the company's philosophy and work ethic.

NEW ENTREPRENEURS

Since the government announced that the economy was finally open to private investment, nearly everyone is a potential entrepreneur. Everyone who is of working age is either about to go into business, has just done so or is about to leave his government job where the pay is so low that it is hardly enough to keep body and soul together. Many do not know how to go about it or where to start but nevertheless take the plunge.

Those who have always had a family business and business connections have the advantage because they can expand and diversify. On the other hand, some of those who worked in government jobs are the ones who may not have connections or capital, and they also lack exposure to business practices. They may also be very cautious and not keen to take risks.

Private limited companies and partnerships are now being registered in quite large numbers. At the same time, the newspapers carry announcements of dissolutions every day. Export-import businesses, in name only, seem to be particularly popular. This may be because passports may be issued to the manager or director of such companies, who can then travel to places within the region to look for business of any kind.

Lack of exposure to the international business environment and business practices is perhaps the greatest drawback these new entrepreneurs face. During all the years that Burma has been closed, the business world has been totally transformed by high technology that most Burmese have no conception of.

Nevertheless, since there are now many young people studying business administration and computer science both within the country and overseas, there is hope for the future. In trying to understand this, one must remember that the Burmese never saw black and white TV but were first introduced to the medium in colour. They are having to cope with the same situation in business.

After some teething troubles, a fledgling class of entrepreneurs and a large number of would-be businessmen and women must inevitably produce successful business people in the near future.

BUSINESS LANGUAGE

English is the language in which business is conducted. Every official will be likely to speak English to a reasonable degree. Contracts will be signed in English. Burmese is necessary only for social purposes, to be able to greet your counterparts. Fluency is not essential.

BUSINESS MEETINGS

Business in Burma is largely on a face-to-face basis so that phone calls will be to no avail (if you can get your call through in the first place). Your counterpart has to see you first before he will even think of doing business and, after seeing you, he may still need to get to know you better.

The first meeting will probably be to literally look at you and find out more about you personally. Then your investment intentions and your expertise will be matched against what is required on the Burmese side. Giving overall summaries rather than greatly detailed plans at first meetings is likely to get your plans understood better.

If you need to meet government officials (as is highly likely since large ventures will probably be government-linked) it is important to get titles of rank and names correct. Ministries are divided into corporations and directorates. Corporations deal in products and directorates in services. Managing Directors and Director Generals are the chief executive officers of corporations and directorates. General Managers, the next level, are the subordinates of Managing Directors. Ministers themselves may participate at meetings.

Women officials may not shake hands with you on being introduced. It is better to wait to see if ladies extend hands first, before making a mistake. Smiles and nods are otherwise sufficient.

Burma Standard Time

Burma Standard Time is "rubber" time. The concept of time is not always related to the clock. Officials can keep you waiting for hours, but visitors should be punctual!

Slowness pervades nearly every process in Burma, especially if it is linked in any way to officialdom. You have to understand that slowness is caused by extreme caution, not wishing to make mistakes,

language problems and trying to gauge trustworthiness, among other reasons. A lot of officials are entrenched in cautiousness from years of working in a system that never rewards initiative and quick action, but punishes every mistake, even when a "mistake" was really the right thing to do.

Greasing palms has been rampant and in inverse proportion to the slowness!

DRESSING ETIQUETTE

Dress code for business meetings is at least a tie and shirt if not full suit. The Burmese will wear an overjacket, called *tike-pon*, to the office and to meetings. Women will wear a long-sleeved blouse to the office. Short sleeves or sleeveless blouses are for casualwear only. Women business visitors should wear skirt suits or trouser suits. Neatness and smartness are valued more than high fashion. Most offices are as yet not air-conditioned so light materials are more suitable than heavy ones.

ENTERTAINING AND GIFTS

Entertaining business friends tends to take place in hotels and restaurants. Official dinners are also held in hotels.

Colleagues generally expect gifts only when they leave an organisation, if they are getting married or having a baby. It is not usual to buy presents for celebrations such as New Year.

In addition to the gift suggestions made in Chapter Five, appropriate gifts for business colleagues are paper weights, diaries, pens, and other kinds of stationery. For working women, handbags and purses are also appropriate.

CULTURAL QUIZ

SITUATION 1

You want to invite a Burmese friend over to an informal dinner at your house. You run into this friend but he is with two other friends whom you know only slightly. You:

A Invite your friend only and ignore the other two.
B Invite the whole group, telling your friend to bring his friends as well.
C Change your mind and decide not to invite any of them.

Comments

The first solution is typical of Westerners who are not acquainted with Burmese ways. By inviting only one person out of a group it shows that you do not value the friendship of the other two - an insult in Burmese eyes. Moreover, it is worth remembering that Burmese like to have a companion when they go to dinners, not necessarily escorts, but simply a familiar Burmese face. This applies especially when they are with foreigners.

The third solution is a possible one, as it is likely that your friend will be reluctant to come alone anyway.

Solution *B* is the best in a Burmese situation because it shows you understand the concept of face. It is likely that two or all three of the group will turn up.

SITUATION 2

The daughter of one of your business friends is getting married. The wedding card has arrived and it says in Burmese at the bottom: "Kindly do not give wedding presents". Your secretary translates this for you, but offers no advice. What does it mean and how would you handle it?

A Ignore the instruction and bring a present anyway.
B Heed the instruction and go to the wedding without a gift.
C Make an excuse not to attend as you feel it puts you under some kind of obligation.

Comments

The little line at the bottom of a wedding card is often seen, especially when couples feel that they do not want to impose on guests for wedding presents at a time when prices of many consumer goods are barely affordable for most.

As you are a friend and wish to maintain the social and business relationship, you should ignore this line and give a present anyway.

It need not be terribly expensive or luxurious but something really useful like bed linen, towels of good quality or a small tea set - something that the bride, especially, will appreciate. *B* would be seen as niggardly on your part if you are well off. *C* is not a good option as not attending without good reason could be taken as an insult.

SITUATION 3

You are about to leave Burma after having stayed there some years. You have some things you would like to dispose of, such as good quality children's clothes, cosmetics, household linen, books and electrical appliances. Some Burmese friends ask you whether you will be selling any of your things. You:

A Tag everything with a price and will not entertain bargaining.
B Price the electrical appliances, but decide to give away some things with each appliance sold.
C Decide to give the clothes and books to Burmese friends who have quite large families, bringing the gifts over to their home yourself.

Comments

B is a good solution because it allows you to earn something without appearing stingy. No one expects you to give away everything. What is more important, you save face for your friends who would not want to receive too much for free. To price everything (*A*) is possible, but you will appear to be miserly and too eager to earn money from used articles!

The third solution is a reasonable option, but before you act on it, you should inquire whether your friends would be interested in the goods. If you are thinking of a group of friends, it is a good idea to lump all the things together for them to divide as they wish. They will then be able to choose what they need.

SITUATION 4

You are going to your country for a home visit. A friend of yours has a son studying abroad. He requests you to take some things which turn out to be quite heavy. You:

A Decide to ring up your friend later and tell him you are unable to carry them with you.

B Decide to take them with your unaccompanied baggage.

C Decide to tell him to take away half of the things and agree to carry the rest.

Comments

A and *C* are solutions that make you appear difficult and ungracious. They also involve a loss of face for you since you have to refuse your friend.

The second solution is a good compromise, as you are not imposed on to the extent of having to carry heavy things yourself. Provided the parcel is not urgently needed, your friend would be happy with this arrangement.

SITUATION 5

You have been travelling around the country with Burmese friends and visit a monastery to take some photographs. The abbot is very kind and shows you old carvings, teak pillars, old statues etc. What should you do when you leave?

A As your Burmese friends pay their respects in the traditional way, you walk out the door.

B You ask your friends if a small donation would be acceptable.

C You shake the monk's hand and thank him.

Comments

The best solution is *B*. It is appropriate for donations to be made after visiting a monastery, whether the abbot has been obliging or not.

As for *C*, you cannot shake hands with a monk if you are a woman: touching the opposite sex is forbidden in their rules.

If you choose *A*, it shows you lack refinement. The abbot has been kind and it is appropriate to show gratitude and respect in some way. It is very rude to go without saying a word, even if you feel confused about how to behave.

GLOSSARY

akutho Opposite of merit, loosely translated as "sin". See *kutho*.

ah-nar-hmu Feeling of not wanting to cause loss of face, pain, not wanting to impose on others.

Abhidhamma The Third Basket of the *Tripitaka* (Basket of Ultimate Things), a subtle analysis of Mind, Psychic Factors, Matter and *Nirvana*. See *Tripitaka*.

aingyi Burmese blouse or shirt.

ba wa Existence.

bhavana Insight or wisdom (Pali).

dana Charity (Pali).

Daw Prefix for adult women.

Eight Precepts See Precepts.

Five Precepts See Precepts.

kadawt Gesture of obeisance made by sitting in a kneeling position on the floor and bowing, with hands held palms together. The *kadawt* is a gesture made to parents and teachers.

Ko Prefix for young adult male.

ko chinn sar-nar-hmu Considerate feeling.

kutho Merit or merits. See *akutho*.

kyat Burmese currency. See *pya*.

longyi Burmese sarong for men and women.

Ma Prefix for young girl.

Maung Prefix for young male.

Precepts Buddhist rules of behaviour. Five Precepts for laymen: abstinence from killing any living thing, from stealing, lying, sexual misconduct and taking intoxicants. Eight Precepts, to be followed on holy days or for the devout: five of the Precepts are the same as above, with refraining from sexual misconduct extended to celibacy. The other three are: refraining from eating meals after noon, from entertainment and adornment of the body, and from sleeping on high and luxurious beds. The Ten Precepts are for monks only. They are the same as the Eight Precepts, except that entertainment and adornment of the body become two separate Precepts, with refraining from handling money added to them.

pya Burmese coins. See *kyat*.

Saya Prefix for teacher, boss, superior (male).

Sayama Prefix for teacher, superior (female).

sila Morality (Pali).

soonkyway Feast for monks.

Ten Precepts See Precepts.

Than-tha-yar Cycles of existence (commonly known as *samsara*).

Tike-pon Over-jacket for men.

Tripitaka Buddhist canon (Three Baskets). See *Abhidhamma*.

Triple Gems Buddha, the *Dhamma* (teachings of Buddha) and the *Sangha* (order of monks).

U Prefix for adult male.

FAMILY TERMS

pe pe ("pay pay")	father
may may	mother
daw daw	aunt
daw lay	younger aunt
u u ("oo oo")	uncle
ba ba	uncle (elder brother of father)
ako, *ako gyi*	elder brother
nyi, *nyi lay*	younger brother
ahma gyi	elder sister
nyi ma lay	younger sister
po po	grandfather
pwa pwa	grandmother
pwa lay	grandaunt

FURTHER READING

Abbott, Gerry, *Back to Mandalay*. Travellers Tales Series, Impact Books, Bromley, Kent, 1990. A delightful account of the author's stay in Mandalay as an English lecturer, ending with the demonstrations of 1988.

Ashin, Thittila (Aggamahapandita), *Essential Themes of Buddhist Lectures*. Department of Religious Affairs, Rangoon, 1987.

Aung San Suu Kyi, *Freedom from Fear*. Penguin Books, New York, 1991. A collection of lucid essays and research papers.

Courtauld, Caroline, *The Collin's Illustrated Guide to Burma*. Collins, London, 1988.

Hla Pe, *Burma: Literature, Historiography, Scholarship, Language, Life and Buddhism*. Institute of Southeast Asian Studies, Singapore, 1985. Lectures, talks and papers given or written as Professor of Burmese at SOAS, University of London. Many aspects of Burmese life are covered, including language, literature, family and Buddhism.

Kingdon Ward, F., *Burma's Icy Mountains*. Jonathan Cape, London, 1949.

Khin Myo Chit, *Colourful Burma*. In two volumes, University Press, 1988. The books cover aspects of Burmese life, from astrology, religion and tradition to trees and Burmese cuisine.

Lewis, Norman, *The Golden Earth*. Jonathan Cape, London, 1952.

Lintner, Bertil, *Outrage: Burma's Struggle for Democracy*. Far Eastern Economic Review Pub. Co., Hong Kong, 1989.

McCrae, Alister, *Scots in Burma: Golden Times in a Golden Land*. Kiscadale Publications, 1990. A good account of Scottish entrepreneurs in the colonial period, covering the Irrawaddy Flottila and the teak, rice, oil and trading businesses.

Mi Mi Khaing, *Burmese Family*. Bloomington, Indiana University Press, 1962. The author's first and most well-known work describes family life in a typical Burmese Buddhist family.

Mi Mi Khaing, *Cook and Entertain the Burmese Way*. First edition, Student Press, 1975. Second edition, Myawaddy Press, 1980. Both books are the only ones published so far in English that have descriptions of common Burmese recipes.

Mi Mi Khaing, *The World of Burmese Women*. Times Books International, Singapore, 1984.

Mya Maung, *The Burma Road to Poverty*. Praeger, 1992.

Mya Maung, *Totalitarian Rule in Burma*. Paragon House, New York, 1993. Analyses the period from 1962 to the present from a political point of view.

O'Brien, Harriet, *Forgotten Land: A Rediscovery of Burma*. Michael Joseph, London, 1991. Impressions of the author on revisiting Burma, the home of her teens.

O'Connor, V.C. Scott, *Mandalay and other cities of the past in Burma*. Hutchison and Co. Paternoster Row, London, 1907. White Lotus Press, Bangkok, 1986. Contains photographs and paintings, as well as a history of the cities visited. Although this book was written about a century ago, the scenes depicted are roughly the same as one would see them today!

Pantoja-Hidalgo, Cristina, *Five Years in a Forgotten Land: A Burmese Notebook*. University of the Philippines Press, Diliman, Quezon City, 1991. Essays written in Burma during travels over the country accompanying her husband, a UNICEF representative. Includes notes on a meeting with Aung San Suu Kyi in 1989.

Pye, Lucian W., *Politics and Nation Building: Burma's Search for Identity*. Yale University Press, 1961. Still relevant in its analysis of Burmese personality and obstacles towards nation building.

Trager, Helen, *We, the Burmese: Voices from Burma*. Praeger, 1969. A collection of articles and essays on aspects of Burmese life.

Vincent Jr., Frank, *Land of the White Elephant (1871–72): Sights and Scenes in Burma, Siam, Cambodia and Cochin China*. London, 1873. White Lotus Press, Bangkok 1988. This book about the American, Frank Vincent's, travels in Burma includes an account of a visit to the Royal Court in Mandalay during the reign of King Maunglon (Mindon).

Yawnghwe, Chao Tzang, *The Shan of Burma*. Institute of Southeast Asian Studies, Singapore, 1987.

THE AUTHOR

SAW MYAT YIN was born in Rangoon (Yangon) in the post-war period. She has lived in Burma most of her life, except for some years abroad studying. She was educated at the Methodist English High School and later at the University of Rangoon. She is married and has two children. Saw Myat Yin is also the author of *Cultures of the World: Burma*, published by Times Editions.

INDEX

Abidhamma 48
address, forms of 91–4
ah-nar-de (*ah-nar-hmu*) 52, 66-7, 101, 112, 113, 178
agriculture 16, 26, 74.
Anglicisation 81, 95–7
animism 51-2
Arakanese 13
arts and literature 81, 109
astrological predictions 38, 59–62, 88, 180
Aung San, General 22, 24
Aung San Suu Kyi 23, 25, 61
Ava 21, 148

banking and finance 183–4
banyan-watering 47
bathing 119–20, 139–40
beds 137–8
black market 11, 26, 73, 74, 80, 84–5, 181
Boat Festival 51
body language 99-107
books 83-4, 173-4
British in Burma 20, 22, 81
Buddhism 21, 33, 35, 39, 42, 43, 54–58, 141
Burmese Empires 21
"Burmeseness" 61
business
    employees 184–9
    favours 179
    language and communica-
    tion 188–9, 190
    legal aspects 182–3
    meetings 191
    networks 180
    relationships 180, 189

calendar (Burmese) 42
cat safes 120
children 33–5, 99, 113
Chin 13, 90
chinlone 109
city-dwellers 73–5
climate 19–20
compliments 115-6
coup d'etat 22, 24, 181

dana 56, 57
demonetisation 25–7, 183
Dhamma 56
domestics 160–5
dress
    for business 192–3
    for eating out 133
    for travel 151–2
    traditional Burmese 104–6
drinks 125
Dry Zone 16

ear-piercing ceremony 33–3
economy 25–8, 180–2
education 28–9, 76, 78–9, 172, 186
Eight Precepts 46, 48
empathy 67
engagements 35
English 95–7
entertaining the Burmese 140–4, 194
environmental perceptions 67–8

Equestrian Festival 51
ethnic groups 11–14
Ethnic War 14

"face" 36, 62, 65–6, 180, 186, 189
family 76–8, 99
feasts 33,111–13
Festival of Lights 48
Five Precepts 71, 74
food
    as a status symbol 129–30
    delicacies 128
    home-cooking 120–1
    jaggery 124, 14
    mee-shay 123
    mohinga 122–3, 131, 143, 178
    ohno-khauk-swe 123
    places to eat 130–2
    rice 127–8
    taboos 128–9
    wet thar dok hto 131
    Western 122
foreign exchange 11, 85–6
Foreign Exchange Certificates 27
foreigners, attitude to 86–7, 114–15
friendship 64–5
fruit 125–6, 149
funerals 32, 39, 42, 101

geography 15–20
gifts 32–3, 37–8, 52–3, 133–5, 156, 193
greetings 94–5

health 171–2
history 20–5
hospitals 38–40, 171-2
housing agents 74–6, 158
Hta-ma-ne festival 50
humour 101–3

Independence 22, 25, 71
insults 41, 98–9, 100
introductions 113–15
Irrawaddy 15, 16–7

Japanese occupation 22, 24
Jataka 50, 110

Kachin 13, 51, 90
kadawt 100
kan (karma) 55–56
Karen 11, 13, 51, 90, 161
Kayah 13
kyat 26, 168

language (Burmese) 97–8
laundry 138
leisure 108–9, 173
Lent (Buddhist) 37, 47
literacy 28–9
longyi 48, 51, 104, 135, 149
lugyone courier 177, 197

make-up 107–8
Mandalay 16, 18, 112, 119, 144, 147–9, 150
Martyrs' Day 22
meals
    conversation at 117–8
    seating at 116–17
    table manners 117–8
    typical meals 121–2
measures 169–70
media 83–4, 86, 108
meditation 57, 58
Mon 13, 20, 90
monks 33–4, 35, 39, 40, 45, 50, 56, 112, 129, 154
months (Burmese) 42–4
Moulmein 18, 147

na yei 31
names 87–9, 114
    difficulties of   90–2
    honorifics   89–90
nat 51, 141
National League for Democracy
    (NLD) 23, 61
Nirvana 57
nouveau riche 18, 85·
novitiation 33–5, 63, 64.

Padaung 14
Pagan
    16, 20, 144, 146, 147, 148, 149, 150, 154
pagodas 147, 154
pandal 45, 46
Panglong Agreement 14, 23, 24
Pegu 21, 147, 148
pets 165–7
photography 35, 37, 75, 154
power supply 159
pregnancy 32, 79
    gifts for 32–3
    taboos and superstitions 32
Prome 20, 147
public holidays 44–5
punctuality
    in business 191–2
    socially 136–7
pwe 48, 110

Rangoon
    12, 18, 112, 119, 130, 131, 148
    climate in 19
    housing in   157–8
    population density in 18
    street names in 18–19
"recycling" 28, 182
Revolutionary Council 23, 25
Robe-Offering 47, 49

Sangha   56
sarong see *longyi*
Shan 11, 13, 90
shinbyu 27, 33
shoes (removing) 75, 152–3
shopping 167–8
    bargaining 170–1
Shway Pyi Daw 10
Shwe Dagon 47, 49, 50, 147
sickness 38–9
Socialist Party 23
    Burmese Way to Socialism 23, 25
sorry 95
sport 109
State Law and Order Restoration
    Council (SLORC) 23, 25
superstition 32, 37, 38, 58, 88, 128

Tazaungdaing 49
Ten Precepts 112
Tenasserim 15, 18, 21, 149
termites 159
tha yei 31
thaing 109
Thakin Movement 22
thanaka 79, 99, 149
thank you 95
Thin gyan 45
toilets 138–40
transport 146, 174–7
Tripitaka 21
Triple Gems 56

villagers 73–4, 75–6
visiting 69–70
    casual visits 135–6
    overnight 136–7

water festival 45
weddings 32, 35, 37, 105, 195
women 64, 78–80, 142, 143